The Hope of Glory

The Hope of Glory

*Exploring the mystery
of Christ in you*

John B. Coburn

A Crossroad Book
THE SEABURY PRESS · NEW YORK

The Seabury Press
815 Second Avenue
New York, N.Y. 10017

Printed in the United States of America

LIBRARY OF CONGRESS CATALOGING IN PUBLICATION DATA

Coburn, John B
  The hope of glory.

  "A Crossroad book."
  1. Protestant Episcopal Church in the U.S.A.—Sermons.
2. Sermons, American. I. Title.
BX5937.C63H66   248′.48′3   75-37751
ISBN 0-8164-1208-1
ISBN 0-8164-2117-X pbk.

Jacket photo of Dr. Coburn by Karsch of Ottowa.

*Dedicated to
the members of the congregation
of St. James Church in New York City
who week by week
attending to the Word
made the speaking
of the Word
possible.*

"How great . . . are the riches of the glory of this mystery, which is Christ in you, the hope of glory."

COLOSSIANS 1:27

Our God is
  the God of *life* who walked the hills of Galilee
  the God of *death* who died on a cross
  the God of *new life* who has been raised beyond
    death
He is known in goodness and beauty and truth,
  and in all that binds men together in friendship
    and love.

Contents

Preface

This book is a development of a central theme in sermons preached at St. James Church, New York, during the years I was rector there from 1969–1975. Whatever truth is in the book comes from the people who listened "in the spirit" and thereby made it possible for me to preach "in the spirit." It reflects, I trust, insights that came to me out of our common life where I gradually discovered that in my ministry to the people of St. James Church it was I who was being ministered to. As I tried to listen to what the spirit was saying to me through my own experiences—failures as well as victories—and to express it in words, the Word—Christ—was heard by those who themselves were likewise trying to live in the spirit. And together we were strengthened.

When in the providence of God, the time came to leave this congregation, I wanted to leave something tangible, a "legacy," as one friend put it. At the same time, another friend, Reid Isaac, senior editor of Crossroad Books, approached me with an invitation to write the Seabury

Lenten Book for 1976. We read together all the sermons I had preached over the six years at St. James Church. It was he (even before I) who identified the basic theme that ran through many of the sermons: the mystery and the glory of Christ's presence within us. He suggested organizing the material under the three headings of Life, Death, and Resurrection; helped structure the sermons into chapters; and introduced clarity where there was confusion. I am deeply grateful for his care and friendship.

The substance of the sermons came from the experiences of the people whose lives I shared—living, dying, being raised, offering up life, its mystery understood and transformed by the spirit. I hope the readers of this book will catch some sense of the "hope of glory" which came to me from those who listened for the Word and made its preaching possible.

September 1975   *John B. Coburn*
New York City

1

The setting

In the Ingmar Bergman film *Scenes from a Marriage*, the wife, Liv Ullmann, is speaking with her husband after he has returned from a trip abroad with another woman. She tries to explain how she was able to begin putting her life back together again when it was shattered by his leaving her and their two children after ten years of a purportedly happy marriage. She says: "The trouble with our marriage was, from my point of view, my inability ever to find out who I was. All I ever was told to do was to please others. And so I tried to please others, especially my parents, and then you, my husband." She went on, "I was determined by other people, and I can't do that anymore. I'm going to determine who I am myself. Now, after this tragic shattering of my life, I have in fact begun to discover who I am and to trust myself. There are three ingredients: I have my common sense, I have my feelings, and I also have my experience. I've been able, in effect, to come to terms with

1

my life and with myself." She has imposed some sense of order on her life.

In the final scene, several years and several lovers later, the couple is asleep and the woman is suddenly awakened by a terrible nightmare. The man wakes up, puts his arm around her, and says, "Tell me, what is the trouble?" "Well," she says, "I was running, and I had my hands out to hold you and our two children, but my hands had disappeared. I had only stumps and I couldn't grab you. And I was sinking in the quagmire." So the man, with his arm around her, says, "Apparently your well-ordered life can't cope with every dimension of your existence." She looks at him and says, "The trouble is I've never been able to love anyone, and no one has ever been able to love me." Then he replies, "Well, I love you, in my inept, selfish way. And you love me in your dominating, demanding way. We *do* love each other—not perfectly, but that's the way we are."

And, by implication, that's the way life is. We somehow have to come to terms with it. The way life is, no matter how we try to impose our order on it, we still have nightmares. No matter how often we run and skip with our hands joined together, there are still times when we only have stumps for arms; we reach out and we can't hold on to anybody; we are sinking into the quagmire. No matter how we love, we never love enough. And our love for others is always intertwined with our love for ourselves. We love ineptly, selfishly, demandingly, dominatingly. That's the way our love is. That's the way we are. That's the way life is—or so it seems.

In fact, it goes deeper than that. Life is terribly ambiguous. We are a body, live in a body, and in the body there is a spirit. We look at life with a certain kind of spirit that is more than our body. We love people, and we use them at the same time. We are loved and we are exploited at the same time. And you don't have to live very long to see that if you are going to affirm life, you have to deal with death. We rejoice in our existence—in our loves and lives and loyalties and friendships—and deep down we know that they're all going to come to an end one day. They don't last.

So, in this ambiguous life, we are anxious. We are anxious to come to terms with life, with ourselves, with the ambiguities and the mixtures we find within ourselves, with the exhilarations and depressions, with the glories and tragedies, with the fulfillments and frustrations, with the beginnings and endings.

Here is a description of how one man came to terms with his life:

. . . outwardly he is completely "a real man." He is a university man, husband and father, an uncommonly competent civil functionary even, a respectable father, very gentle to his wife and carefulness itself with respect to his children. And a Christian? Well, yes, he is that too after a sort; however, he preferably avoids talking on the subject. . . . He very seldom goes to church, because it seems to him that most parsons really don't know what they are talking about. He makes an exception in the case of one particular priest of whom he concedes that he knows what he is talking about, but he doesn't want to hear him for another reason, because he has a fear that this might lead him too far.[1]

Does this sound familiar? Does this describe anybody you know? It describes a man Søren Kierkegaard knew and wrote about back in 1848. He was describing how we erect defenses against the terrifying aspects of life, the deep anxieties and ambiguities and contradictions of our existence.

Somehow we have to deal with the mysterious paradox of who we are. With one side of our nature, we belong to the animal world. We are born, we reproduce, and we die just as everyone in the animal world does. Yet we also have a curious way of looking at this life, a way that arises out of our minds and out of the spirit we bring to examine this life. We are in nature, and we are more than nature. We can fly to the moon and we can also write a poem about the moonlight. We can sing songs and paint pictures. We can make love—spiritual love as well as physical love. We can, in fact, sacrifice our bodies because of our spirits and our loyalties in the spirit. We are creators—and yet we are also creatures. We are at times dispirited, depressed, dishonest, disoriented, defeated creatures. We are both creators and creatures, angels and beasts, glorious and tragic, living and dying.

Both Kierkegaard and Bergman describe how we tend to settle for life on a mediocre level, imposing our order upon it. No great loves, but then no great betrayals either. No lofty exaltations, but then no crushing defeats. Not much life, not all of the life we know we're meant to have, but then we're going to die anyway.

Temporizing, compromising mediocrity is one way in which we deal with this paradoxical nature of ours. It probably is the way that most of us in our secular, middle-class culture try to get through life.

There are two other ways. One is that instead of trying to hold our two natures together, we try to settle for one or the other. Some people try to repudiate the spirit and to dwell on the body, to find meaning in their food or drink or sexual liaisons or material possessions—a modern form of "Let us eat, drink, and be merry, for tomorrow we die." The other way is to deny the body and its demands and satisfactions and requirements. Those who take this way say: "We're going to express our spirit; We're going to be loyal to our spiritual nature and that pure, crystal-clear exaltation of who we are under God. We are going to live on that level and deny the body." This kind of a body/spirit split becomes what we call "schizoid." We end up in breaking down if we deny either our body or our spirit. We can no more settle for bodily satisfactions on the one hand, than we can jump out of our skins on the other. We have to deal with the ambiguous nature that we are.

So there we are—both body and spirit. There is a touch of the angel about us as well as a touch of the beast. We obey the law of self-preservation and we ache to give up our lives to someone we love. We can walk on the moon with huge packs of electronic instruments on our backs, and we can skip crazily naked along the beach in the moonlight. We can see the moon through a telescope and sing a love song to our beloved by its light. Who are *we* that we can do all these things?

What does it all *mean?* If we can find no satisfying or enduring answers in either body or spirit, where can we find them? What do you make of this? How do you answer this question for yourself? Who do you think you are, deep down inside, and what do you think you mean? Where do you feel you belong? When do you feel at home? Whose are you? Anybody's? Or are you, when all is said and done, just utterly alone?

Well, of course, nobody can answer these questions for anybody else. We can see how others answer them, or try to, and be helped in our own struggle, but finally we have to make our own decisions for ourselves—and then live with them.

The answer that the Christian faith has given—or rather the framework within which Christian men and women have wrestled with these questions and given their personal answers—is that the response has to be made to God. The ambiguities of life require the response to be made to someone above and beyond these ambiguities. Life, by itself, doesn't hold the answer. That is why life for so many is senseless, boring, or unbearable. To live in relationship to God, who is above the ambiguities, makes life bearable, however (and we have to settle just for that sometimes), at other times joyful, ecstatic even, and at all times (even the worst times) gives life some meaning. *We mean* something in relationship to God—so we can affirm ourselves.

Can you believe that? If you can say: "Well, I'm not so sure, but I'd like to try," that is a decision for faith. That faith relationship, responding to God (or trying to) with all the contributions of our human nature, is what the Christian religion is about. It is to trust a spirit beyond our spirit, which moves through our spirit, and to try to live in accordance with it. If you can say to yourself, "I'd like to trust that spirit," then all you have to do is to say to God, "I'd like to trust *you.*" That is an act of faith.

If you can say, "I want to trust his spirit moving through my life and my relationships. I want to trust life a little more, to love people a little more, to affirm people a little more, to care for them, and to provide some better kind of justice for those I cannot touch personally," then you have decided for faith. If you can say, "At least in my best moments I am in that spirit, and I trust that spirit to carry me over all the ambiguities and contradictions and broken relationships in life, including that of death," then you have made an act of faith.

That is what Liv Ullmann and her husband were not able to say. People who are flat out in our culture, who have no vertical dimension to their lives, but who are flat out in relationship *only* to one another and to their bodies and their twisted spirits, cannot say that. To say it requires an act of faith, a decision that something more is going on than is visible, and to trust it.

That closing scene in the movie is utterly honest in its realism, it is quite touching in its mutual human accepting of incomplete love, of incomplete selves—but it is finally hopeless, of course. An ending with hope would be: "What little love we do have, and however twisted it may be, we shall now trust to the best of our ability. We shall commit ourselves to love the spirit, and to love each other, who bear the spirit. That is our faith. We will act on it." The ending might not have been any happier, but it would have been filled with hope.

In this book I have tried to point to the ground of the hope that sustains us in the experiences of living and dying and living again. It is the Christ who comes into our setting, who is discovered in the mystery of our lives. Our faith is not in our hope for a more glorious life. It is, rather, in him who already is in us and among us. He is our hope of glory.

PART I

In Life

2

Golden strings

Have you ever sat alone under a tree in the country with quiet all around you and been content just to sit? Have you ever heard the stillness broken with the sound of fluttering and, looking up, seen the branches brushing against each other and the leaves nodding? And have you wondered where the breeze has come from? When the sound stops, have you wondered where it has gone?

Or, as you were sitting under a tree, have you ever crawled on your hands and knees to the base of the trunk and leaned against it? Have you ever closed your eyes and pressed back against the bark and wondered if you could move inside the bark and merge with the tree itself? Have you ever concentrated on being a tree, wondering what it's like to be rooted and grounded . . . sturdy . . . stretching . . . bending?

Have you ever walked through a meadow on a hill at dusk and looked out over a valley? Have you ever sunk slowly to the ground, buried your face in the grass, and smelled the clover and the earth? When you raised your head did you feel the wind blowing down over the hillside? Did you ever sit up, pull some blades of grass, put them in your mouth and chew them? And as you looked out over the valley, and twilight slowly gathered, did it seem sometimes as though a sudden hush had settled over the world, almost as though the earth stood still for a moment?

Did you ever at such moments as these have a sense of being caught up in the world of nature, a world that was there before you came and will be there long after you have gone, a world that has its own being and integrity, a world that is going about its own business quite independently of you, a world which in turn seems to be reflecting a world beyond itself, as though something else were going on that had its own nature, a nature which you could not fathom but could recognize and acknowledge? Then later, when you walked back down the hill, spitting out the chewed-up grass, were you perhaps a little more reflective, a little more thoughtful, a little more buoyant than you had been, as though you had been invited into another world and been given a fleeting glimpse of what goes on in that world, as though you had brushed up against something different, other-worldly, passing over your spirit? And so *you* were different.

Have you ever had such experiences as these? Most of us have, sometime in our lives; most young people do, sometimes with great intensity. I hope you remember them—even better, I hope you still have them. They can be cultivated or, more accurately, you can put yourself in the way of them. They are part of our fundamental, essential humanity, our common human heritage, where through the world of nature we are put in touch with mystery.

It is the recognition of that mystery—sometimes its worship—that helps keep us human, makes us more

human, and sometimes even more than human. There are
moments when we are suddenly aware of, or at least we
suspect, a world beyond our world, beyond our physical
world; a spirit that is related to—and yet is more
than—our spirit; a mysterious movement about us that
compels our attention and seems to tantalize and tempt
us; to point to, draw us to, introduce us to another realm
even more real than the one we live in.

So let us continue this exploration. In Kenneth Grahame's *The Wind in the Willows*, there are two good
friends, Rat and Mole. They discover one day that a young
friend of theirs, the baby otter, has been lost. So they set
out in their boat on the river to try to find him. They go
upstream poking along the river bank, calling for him
from time to time. The day goes by, darkness falls, soon
the moon comes out and in the light of the moon they
continue to pull and to poke and to call. Then in time the
moon begins to sink. Soon it disappears into the earth.
Darkness descends, black and mysterious. Then in the
predawn hush a change begins to take place along the
river.

The horizon became clearer, field and tree came more into
sight, and somehow with a different look; the mystery began to
drop away from them. A bird piped suddenly, and was still; and
a light breeze sprang up and set the reeds and bulrushes
rustling. Rat, who was in the stern of the boat, while Mole
sculled, sat up suddenly and listened with a passionate intent-
ness. Mole, who with gentle strokes was just keeping the boat
moving while he scanned the banks with care, looked at him
with curiosity.

He hears something. Then he loses it. Then it comes
again.

"O Mole! the beauty of it! The merry bubble and joy, the thin,
clear, happy call of the distant piping! Such music I never
dreamed of, and the call in it is stronger even than the music is

sweet! Row on, Mole, row! For the music and the call must be for us!''

So, in silence, Mole rows steadily on. Then he, too, hears the distant piping. It breaks upon him, catches him up, and possesses him. It brings both pain and joy. The sound grows nearer. The boat comes to rest on the shore of an island.

"This is the place of my song-dream, the place the music played to me," whispered the Rat, as if in a trance. "Here, in this holy place, here if anywhere, surely we shall find Him!"

Then suddenly the Mole felt a great Awe fall upon him, an awe that turned his muscles to water, bowed his head, and rooted his feet to the ground. It was no panic terror—indeed he felt wonderfully at peace and happy—but it was an awe that smote and held him and, without seeing, he knew it could only mean that some august Presence was very, very near. With difficulty he turned to look for his friend, and saw him at his side cowed, stricken, and trembling violently. And still there was utter silence in the populous bird-haunted branches around them; and still the light grew and grew.

Perhaps he would never have dared to raise his eyes, but that, though the piping was now hushed, the call and the summons seemed still dominant and imperious. He might not refuse, were Death himself waiting to strike him instantly, once he had looked with mortal eye on things rightly kept hidden. Trembling he obeyed, and raised his humble head; and then, in that utter clearness of the imminent dawn, while Nature, flushed with fullness of incredible colour, seemed to hold her breath for the event, he looked in the very eyes of the Friend and Helper; saw the backward sweep of the curved horns, gleaming in the growing daylight; saw the stern, hooked nose between the kindly eyes that were looking down on them humorously, while the bearded mouth broke into a half-smile at the corners; saw the rippling of the muscles on the arm that lay across the broad chest, the long supple hand still holding the pan-pipes only just then fallen away from the parted lips; saw the splendid curves of the shaggy limbs disposed in majestic ease on the sward; saw, last of all, nestling between his very hooves, sleeping soundly in entire peace and contentment, the little, round, podgy, childish form of the baby otter. All this he saw, for one moment breathless and intense, vivid on the morning sky; and still, as he looked, he lived; and still, as he lived, he wondered.

"Rat!" he found breath to whisper, shaking. "Are you afraid?"

"Afraid?" murmured the Rat, his eyes shining with unutterable love. "Afraid! Of *Him?* O, never, never! And yet—and yet—O, Mole, I am afraid!"

Then the two animals, crouching to the earth, bowed their heads and did worship.

Sudden and magnificent, the sun's broad golden disc showed itself over the horizon facing them; and the first rays, shooting across the level water-meadows, took the animals full in the eyes and dazzled them. When they were able to look once more, the Vision had vanished, and the air was full of the carol of birds that hailed the dawn.[1]

So the story—and the experiences. You see and hear the fluttering leaves; you feel the breeze that comes, goes; you press back into the trunk of a tree; you watch twilight fall over the valley. And should you be asked, "Friend, are you afraid?" you might answer with Rat, "Afraid! Of Him? O, never, never! And yet—and yet—O, Mole, I am afraid!" And then you might, with them, bow your head and worship.

These experiences are "Golden Strings"—described by William Blake in this verse:

> I give you the end of a golden string
>   Only wind it into a ball,
> It will lead you in at heaven's gate,
>   Built in Jerusalem's wall.[2]

The Golden String: the stillness, the breeze, the smell, the crash of surf. Golden Strings are let down through the world of nature by God. Where is your Golden String? Take it from God, wind it. "It will lead you in at heaven's gate, built in Jerusalem's wall."

3

Beauty and the humiliated

When I taught in the Street Academy in Harlem in 1968, the second most popular book was *The Prophet* by Kahlil Gibran. That was a great surprise to me. The most popular book was *The Autobiography of Malcolm X.* That was no surprise. Malcolm X spoke to the condition of those students, how they lived, how they hustled, the work they had or did not have, the crime they committed, the prisons they knew, the drugs they carried. It was an extraordinary experience to read, through the eyes of black young people, that book by a man who had lived as they had lived, who gave himself for his people, and who, toward the end of his life, had hope for work with white people. It was not difficult to understand the appeal of *Malcolm X.*

But the popularity of *The Prophet* was another matter. Of all the religious and pseudo-religious books I have read, (and I have read more than my sins deserve), *The Prophet* would have been the last book I would have recommended to black young people on the streets of

Harlem. In my judgment, its appeal was sentimental and romantic. It had a version of semi-religious mystical experience that may have some basis in reality in heaven, but certainly was not grounded in life on the earth.

To be sure, it has been popular for a long time. It has a great appeal to adolescents, and, as an adolescent, I loved it and memorized parts of it. But when I became a man (theologically speaking), educated and mature, I put away adolescent things, including such things as *The Prophet*. Certainly, in my judgment, it could mean nothing to tough kids educated on the streets of New York.

I could not have been more wrong. The book did speak to those young people. It was introduced to the class by a young girl, a mother who worked four hours at night after spending all day in school. She said, "Last summer I read that book, and that was a beautiful book. I think our class would like to read it."

So they read it and they did like it. It spread to other classes and apparently elsewhere, because I finally gave away twice as many books as there were students enrolled in the school. It was—and this is the word they kept using—beautiful.

There was one nineteen-year-old boy, son of a black father and a white mother. He had been on his own since he was nine years old, living anywhere, moving around that year in dormitories at New York University. He would come a half hour early every morning for three weeks just to read *The Prophet*. He could read, but he could not write a sentence. He was tall, ungainly, not very personable. He cut his own hair—apparently about twice a year. He had tennis sneakers on his feet in February and no socks. He wore dungarees and an army field jacket. His schooling was erratic, and he was a hustler. But he could read, and one morning he read this:

And a poet said, Speak to us of Beauty.
And he answered:

Where shall you seek beauty, and how shall you find her unless
    she herself be your way and your guide?
And how shall you speak of her except she be the weaver of
    your speech?
The aggrieved and the injured say, "Beauty is kind and gentle.
Like a young mother half shy of her own glory she walks among
    us."
And the passionate say, "Nay, beauty is a thing of might and
    dread.
Like the tempest she shakes the earth beneath us and the sky
    above us."
The tired and the weary say, "Beauty is of soft whisperings. She
    speaks in our spirit.
Her voice yields to our silences like a faint light that quivers in
    fear of the shadow."
But the restless say, "We have heard her shouting among the
    mountains.
And with her cries came the sound of hoofs, and the beating of
    wings and the roaring of lions."

All these things have you said of beauty,
Yet in truth you spoke not of her but of needs unsatisfied,
And beauty is not a need but an ecstasy.
It is not a mouth thirsting nor an empty hand stretched forth,
But rather a heart enflamed and a soul enchanted.
It is not the image you would see nor the song you would hear,
But rather an image you see though you close your eyes and a
    song you hear though you shut your ears.
It is not the sap within the furrowed bark, nor a wing attached
    to a claw,
But rather a garden forever in bloom and a flock of angels
    forever in flight.
People of Orphalese, beauty is life when life unveils her holy
    face.
But you are life and you are the veil.
Beauty is eternity gazing at itself in a mirror
But you are eternity and you are the mirror.[3]

When he finished reading, he looked up and said, "I dig
that. That is beautiful."

I said, "Carlos, do you think that it is true that there is a
way of beauty?"

"God, I don't know. But, Mr. Coburn, there has *got* to be. There has just *got* to be. But I don't know."

After three weeks he disappeared. I never saw him again. I will never forget him.

The recognition of beauty by the beaten ones, the yearning for beauty by the humiliated, the hope in beauty by those who have almost no cause for hope is a great mystery. There is beauty, but it may not be true. "No," he says, "it has just *got* to be." Beauty—a part of the life of the afflicted, the dispossessed, those who have hope unless and until hope gets driven out.

What a mystery! What a mystery that beauty is affirmed by the afflicted. With my own ears I have heard this mystery affirmed by poor blacks in New York City.

Listen now to the voices of poor whites. These are voices from Appalachia recorded by Dr. Robert Coles, a research psychiatrist at Harvard who marvels at the way beauty and faith are valued by some who are often described as "poor wretched believers." These words are by a woman for whom believing is more important than poverty or wretchedness:

I wait all week for Sunday. That's the day that counts, you know. It's the only day of the week for me, the only one when *we* count, because then God is there beckoning you, telling you that it's all right. Just come on over and be with me, be with me for a few minutes. Yes, sir, if you do, if you go to him, if you be with him, then, like he says, you'll be all right. . . .

And another, a migrant worker:

I kneel all week long with the beans, but on Sunday I kneel to speak with God, and he makes my knees feel better, much better. . . . On Sundays I have to go thank someone, thank him for giving me the strength. He must—must—want you. He must be thinking of you, not just of everyone else, or how could I still be going, going as strong as I am?

A woman describes why she is about to walk two miles to church under a hot sun:

I know it'll be worth it, because it always is. I get tired and my feet are aching bad—the shoes, you know—but once I'm there I can forget me and my feet and everything, because there's Someone up there, and he's bigger than all of us, and if you know that, once you do, then you're on your way, and it won't be long before every one of us will be there, meeting him, and what he decides is what counts, and nothing else. I get discouraged a lot by things; there'll be this to bother you, or something else again. (You're not put here to have an easy time, I guess.) When I'm low, I'll wonder if there's any point—you know—to going on. But that's only temporary. I'll be setting there and hearing the minister, and we'll be singing, and all of a sudden there's God talking to me. I know he is. It's not that he'll say anything special. No, sir. It's just that I can feel the truth; it's there, and it's big enough that I can rely on the message. . . .

To me church is where you meet God, where for a little while you find him and keep him, where he tells you that it's all right, and it's going to be all right, and no matter what, you'll come out on his side—if you want to—and sets it on your mind that you will. I'll let you in on a secret; it's not him, the minister who does the convincing of me. It's God and how he does it, I don't know . . . it's not that someone has come along and promised to help you out. I guess if I had to say—it's hard to say these things, you know—then I'd say it's like you're under a cloud, a real bad one, and the sun is gone and it's raining, and maybe some thunder and lightning are there. But all quick-like, you see the sky clear up, and not only is there the sun to see, but it's cool too, at the same time, and you've got a nice friendly world around you, over you, protecting you and keeping you warm. But you don't go and get too warm. And the crops, they're growing like mad, and they'll be easy to pick, because they'll get nice and dried out. So you feel good, and you know you've found your rest. And you look around and you see there's others; they've been saved too.

I don't know much about being saved . . . but there will be a little while on Sundays—not all Sundays, no, but some of them —when I feel real good. The uplift, it's got me hoping. I'll be hoping the week will be better, and I'll not have the pains I get in my stomach; but mostly it'll be I'll have a better spirit about everything. . . . That's how I think.[4]

That's how she thinks. "The uplift has got me hoping . . . mostly it'll be that I'll have a better spirit about everything."

That is how some poor whites think. Out of affliction, hope; out of poverty, a better spirit; out of back-breaking work, an affirmation of beauty. Is it true? You have heard her. That is how she thinks. She says it's true. What do you think? I think there's not much difference between the young man in Harlem saying about beauty, "It's got to be true," and this woman saying, "The uplift's got me hoping." I also think that there is not much difference between their hope and my hope. Both of us hope in something other than man and both of us call it God.

But there is a difference. They are the afflicted in our society, and I am not. They are the poor, and I am not. They are the powerless, and I am not. Yet it is the same God we approach, and at the same altar we receive the same broken body of him who was afflicted for our sakes. In him is our hope.

Albert Camus was a noble spirit who dealt with the great issues of our day, of what it is to be a man in the twentieth century in a troubled, affluent, poverty-stricken world. He knew the grandeur and tragedy of the human spirit. He was possessed by that spirit, and it was reflected in his own life and in his own "uplift" that kept him hoping. Here is what he thought about the mystery that we have been discussing:

"There is beauty and there are the humiliated. Whatever difficulties the enterprise may present, I would like never to be unfaithful to the one or the other."

This word from one who did not believe in God seems close to the Word of God for me.

There is beauty and there are the humiliated. Whatever difficulties the enterprise may present we would like never to be unfaithful to one or the other.

4

On being a little crazy

Light! Light! Light!
Lifted
Living
Life

That is a prayer. You might say, "That doesn't sound like a prayer to me. That sounds rather like a simple spontaneous utterance. It's an expression of an inner mood. It's the stirring of the spirit within, that from time to time simply has to burst forth in some kind of expression."

It's the sort of thing you say when, at one moment, everything seems suddenly to fall into place. It's when every aspect of your life miraculously seems absolutely right. You don't feel sorry for yourself. You don't hold any grievances. Whatever tasks you are called upon to perform, you know you will be able to do them. Or if you can't say that, at least you know you are going to be able

22

to do all you can do, and you're not going to agonize over what you can't do. At that moment you sense that your life is moving with unusual direction and power and spirit. There is a rightness about it, a fulfillment and a completion, and you say, "What a day! What a day!"

Such a filled moment is a happening. That is, it just happens. It just comes. Something lights a spark within you. Suddenly, a flame seems to flare up. It becomes a blaze and bursts into some kind of glory. It may be a book that triggers it, or a poem or a movie or a look or a letter or a handshake. It may be an event remembered—like a child tumbling somersaults in the leaves in the park and walking away with his hand in his father's, the leaves hanging on his sweater like medals of valor. He skips, and his father skips, too. Anyway, whatever sparks it, all of a sudden you are alive and you say, "What a day!" Or perhaps you say,

> *Light! Light! Light!*
> *Lifted*
> *Living*
> *Life*

When you are in such a mood, it doesn't mean your troubles go away. It means you know you can live with them; perhaps you can resolve some of them; in any case, they are not going to get you down. They are not in charge of you. Something else is.

When you say with such exuberance, "What a day!" it doesn't mean that you aren't going to have any more bad days. You know there are going to be days when nothing works, when you will again be down, and you will wonder if you can just hang on and get through the day. You know you're not going to get your way all the time; but when you're in this kind of a mood, you don't have your heart set on getting your way anyway.

Your heart is set on what is happening to you. The happening—the sense of being caught up, almost of being set upon, of being carried, lifted, propelled, the glimmer of delight and wonder and joy—that happening is all-important. You might not say it to anybody else, but to yourself you say, "This is glorious. It's a glorious day because what's happening to me is glorious."

Of course, you can't *make* it happen. There's nothing you can do to bring this about. It has nothing to do with whether you deserve it and are a good person or not. You don't earn it. It just comes. At such a moment, your spirits are suddenly lifted and you know you are all right. Life is all right; life, in fact, is glorious. And again, though you might not say it even to yourself, you sense in a curious way that *you* are glorious.

I hope you have had experiences like this. But you might say, "I don't have experiences like that. That's crazy." As a matter of fact, it probably is a little crazy. Anybody who tries to be a Christian has to be a little crazy. Anybody who says, "The things in life that I can't see are more important than the things in life that I can see," is bound to appear a little deranged. It doesn't make much sense to say that the glorious happenings that burst upon you when your spirit simply sings are eternal. But that is what Christians *do* say, and that is what they believe. They don't say they are crazy; they say they have *faith:*

—faith that integrity and honesty and moral courage and forgiveness and sacrifice are infinitely more important than money, cars, homes, savings accounts, or anything else.

—faith that what happens to a person's spirit is infinitely more important than what happens to his body.

—faith that the question, "Is it true?" is infinitely more important than the question, "Can I get away with it?"

—faith that what happens to my neighbor is just as important as what happens to me.

—faith that my destiny and the destiny of my family and the destiny of my kind is intertwined inexorably and eternally with the destiny of those who are not my kind, who are different in color or class or creed.

It sounds crazy, but the Christian fact is that the law of life is the law of love; and if you can't love, at least you can let the glory happen to you.

You have to be a little crazy to make sense out of an irrational world. That's how the Christian interprets the mystery of existence, how he deals with the tragedy and the glory of mankind together—the heights and the depths, the greatness and the nobility of the human spirit as well as its viciousness and meanness. You have to be a little crazy to deal with the things of the earth, earthly and mortal, and say that they are part and parcel of things which are eternal and immortal.

That's why the words

Light! Light! Light!
Lifted
Living
Life

are a prayer. They are a prayer because they are addressed by faith to God. When the experiences you have in life are caught up and expressed to God in words, that's a prayer. The experiences themselves, when they are directed to God, become a prayer. In fact, when you do this, *you* become a prayer. You don't need the words, you need only the experiences. You need only take the happenings that come and give them back to God.

All the experiences that you go through in life make most sense when they are lived in God. Then all the happenings—the inglorious ones as well as the moving, noble ones—go from glory to glory, and so do *you*. That is your eternal destiny and you live it right now.

Crazy, isn't it?

> *Light! Light! Light!*
> *Lifted*
> *Living*
> *Life*
> *Christ, the true light*
> *Eternal Life*
> *You.*

Amen.

5

Recognizing the presence of God

"The place on which you stand is holy ground."

So God spoke to Moses and so he speaks to us today. "The place on which you stand is holy ground."

To get there, to the original holy ground, you have to leave Cairo at three o'clock in the afternoon, spend the night in Suez, leave Suez the following morning at three o'clock in a caravan of not less than three cars, cross the canal by ferry, turn right and go down the western side of the Sinai Peninsula. (That was how it was before the Six Day War of 1967.)

Halfway down the peninsula you turn left, eastward, and begin a whole day's journey across the trackless desert. By noon it is so hot you can't put your hand on the outside of the car because it sizzles. When the car is stuck in the sand and you get out and push, perspiration pours over you.

The stop at the oasis in the middle of the afternoon brings tea, shade, and rest from the bucking car. Re-

27

freshed, you continue mile after mile over utterly desolate land, stark and godforsaken, without life of any kind. In the distance from time to time, you see Bedouins driving their flocks before them.

Finally, just before sunset there rises the mountain range called Sinai at the very southern tip of the peninsula. Coming closer, you see nestled at the base of the mountain what seems to be a walled castle. That is the Monastery of St. Catherine founded in the reign of Justinian. It is the goal of your journey, for centuries a place of pilgrimage and of prayer. With entrance into that monastery, the cooling breeze of the desert night air drives away the stifling heat of the day.

The monastery stands above a crypt where the Chapel of the Burning Bush is built. It is the place where, according to legend, Moses saw a bush burned, and it was not burned up. Here is where this Israelite refugee from the slave camp in Egypt was a shepherd 1300 years before Christ was born. One day he was following his sheep through the wilderness when he saw a bush that was burning but wasn't consumed. Curious and somewhat frightened, he turned aside and drew near, fascinated to see why the burning did not consume the bush.

As he watched, he heard a voice, "Moses, don't come any nearer. Take your shoes off. The ground you are standing on is holy."

Frightened and still, he heard the voice say, "I have watched the suffering of the Israelites. I have heard their appeal to be free. I want you to go back to Egypt. Go back; gather them together. Tell Pharaoh you are leading them out of Egypt. I want you to lead those people into a land flowing with milk and honey."

Moses replied, "How can I, a shepherd, speak like this to a Pharaoh? How can I do this?"

The voice said, "You can do it, because I am doing it."

"Well," said Moses, "if I go to the people of Israel and

tell them that this is what I am going to do, what shall I
say about the authority that I have? Who sent me? What
shall I say his name is?"

"You can say, 'I am who I am' sent you.

Or you can say, 'I am what I am' sent you.

Or you can say, 'I will be what I will be' sent you.

Or you can simply say, 'I am' sent you.

You can say, 'The Lord, the God of your fathers, the
God of Abraham, the God of Isaac, the God of Jacob has
sent me—that which is and that which causes all to be
sent me'."

"So go, Moses. Go to Pharaoh and say, 'Let my people
go!' I promise you; you will do it, because I am doing it. I
want them set free."

So he went, and he did. He took his stand on holy
ground. There on that ground where he found himself, he
was caught up in an experience that came to him. It came
out of the wilderness, initiated by some power other than
his own power. It frightened him and fascinated him,
drew him and yet held him at a distance. It possessed him
even as he was protesting. Then when he acted, he struck
a blow for freedom.

These seem to be the qualities necessary in human life
to recognize the presence of God—necessary in our lives
if we are to have any insights into discerning the ground
we stand on as holy ground.

Your holy ground is the ground of your being when you
finally take your stand and say, "I am." "I am who I am. I
am what I am. I am me. I am nobody else. I am not what
other people try to make me. I am not what other people
want me to be. I am no longer concerned about the image
I project, whether I am getting along or not getting along.
I am no longer going to try to pretend to be someone I am
not. I am through pretending, covering, living, if not a lie,
not quite the whole truth. I am myself, uniquely, wholly
myself, and nobody else. So I accept myself as I am with

all my failures as well as hopes, too many sins as well as too few virtues, all my spiritual life as well as my physical life; I am going to be me.

"To do this, to grow in becoming myself, I'll try to be alert to those experiences that mystify me and frighten me and fascinate me. I'll try to respond to those as fully as I can. And if there are fears that come, I will listen to those fears; and if there are anxieties, I'll track those anxieties down and see where they come from. And if I am exposed to something that I believe is deeply true, I will try to respond and live in accordance with that truth. And as God gives me to know the right, God help me, I will try to live in accordance with that right and nothing else.

"That is to be put in touch with the growing edge of my life. Rather than running from pain when it comes, I'll try to accept it. If I am in trouble, I'll face it, and I'll go through the trouble and make the decisions I have to make. I will be responsible for myself.

"I'll listen to those voices, the experiences that call me by name to become more wholly myself. So I'll live with a little more wonder; and I'll live a little bit more deeply in touch with the mystery of life, sensing the awesomeness and, at times, even the glory of it."

When Moses left, he left for Egypt. He left for Egypt to set his people free. His acts were acts of freedom. God's acts are acts of freedom. You can act to set people free, because God acts to set people free. God is freedom.

You can set yourselves free from whatever binds you, from whatever you are a slave to. You don't have to be fettered the rest of your life. You can be set free from the tyrannies that shackle you. You can be free of self-pity, of rage, of passions—passions to outdo everybody else, to be possessed by money or prestige or making the scene. Those are binding fetters.

Setting others free is part of being free ourselves.

Setting others free from that which binds them—particularly setting them free from us if we, in our relationship to them, are treating them as though we possessed them, as though they were our own, as though they lived for our life rather than on their own ground and in their own being. We will set those we love free to find themselves on the ground that they choose—not on our ground.

Those you cannot set free personally, but who are bound in our society, you set as free as you can. Those fellow members of this society who are bound slaves to poverty, who live under the tyranny of rats in their houses, and who are bound by the viciousness of hate because other people have a different color, you set free where and how you can. None of us is free as long as anyone is in prison—particularly anyone whom we can set free—shackled either by our own bonds or the bonds of society. When we move to help men become free, the ground we stand on becomes holy. We can do it if we want to do it, because God does it.

So how do you recognize the presence of God? It is recognized only as it is practiced. If there is no act toward freedom, there is no Presence. A conviction comes to you in your life, perhaps right out of the blue, or perhaps just a gnawing, insistent voice that grows louder and louder within you, that you must do something more than you have done before to help yourself become free, and to set another person free. As you respond to that conviction, you are practicing the presence of God.

So who are the people in this world that you can help become a little freer by something you can do today? When you do it, you will be practicing the presence of God. And if they should say to you, "Why are you doing this? Who is sending you? What is its name, or his name?" you can say, "*I am* sends me. Life sends me. The Lord sends me. The God of our fathers, the God of Abraham and of Isaac and of Jacob, the God of Our Lord Jesus Christ sends me. *I am* sends me. That is his name."

6

On riding motorcycles

One of the happiest memories of my childhood—which, on the whole, was a happy one—is of motorcycle rides. A young man in our neighborhood owned a motorcycle and on summer evenings he would stop by the porch where I was sitting with other members of our family, and he would say, "Want a ride?" Would I! Finally, with my parents' permission—a debate each time he asked the question—he would lift me, then four or five years old, on to the front saddle. He would sit behind me and put his hands on the handle bars, locking me safely in, turn the throttle, race the motor, and off we would go in a cloud of dust. We whipped dangerously around the corners at what seemed a thousand miles an hour. We went like the wind, and as Tom Swift used to say, "the motorcycle ate up the road."

Exciting and exhilarating! Nothing quite like it. The words: "Harley Davidson" were noble words that lifted one's heart as much as other words of that time: Babe Ruth, Yankee Stadium, and Lou Gehrig!

During my freshman year at college the dream of owning a motorcycle finally came true. My roommate and I bought a secondhand motorcycle in Philadelphia for twenty-five dollars. We had to forge the name of a friend, because it was against the rule for undergraduates in those days to have motorcycles or automobiles. We forged his name with his permission because we were going to store the motorcycle in his barn.

The drive from Philadelphia brought a sense of ecstasy and freedom that was all we had anticipated, and more. For several weeks we would hitchhike out to Hopewell where we kept the motorcycle. We would then spin around the countryside exulting in life as only college freshmen can, especially when there is also the thrill of knowing you are breaking the law and getting away with it!

One Sunday afternoon the motorcycle broke down. We had not the slightest idea how to put it together again, nor how to care for it—nor, I suppose, any real desire to learn. It was too technical a proposition for us; we concentrated on Latin poets in those days. No garage was open, so we pushed the motorcycle the four or five miles from Lawrenceville to Hopewell. We sold it the following week for twenty-five dollars, and I haven't been on a motorcycle since.

I mention this fascinating data of my autobiography in order to establish my credibility as a commentator upon the book, *Zen and the Art of Motorcycle Maintenance* by R. M. Persig. It is one of the most interesting, unusual, and profound discussions of the world of ideas and of values that I have ever read. It is, in my judgment, an absolute *tour de force* wherein the author develops the concepts of knowledge, self-knowledge, right and wrong, and meaning in an absolutely fresh way. Without any of the traditional religious words, it is as religious a book as

I have read in a long time and infinitely more interesting than most.

The author of *Zen and the Art of Motorcycle Maintenance* is a middle-aged college professor who has lost his job. He rides his motorcycle through the Northwest from Montana to the Pacific Coast with his teen-aged son on the back seat. Sometimes their relationship is warm and friendly, mutually understanding and supportive; at other times, they are estranged, alienated, do not understand each other, and hurt each other.

The father has been alienated within himself. He has had a breakdown and been in a mental hospital, and tries to understand that thin line between rationality and irrationality. He is a motorcycle buff, knows everything about motorcycles, loves his motorcycle, loves to keep the engine in perfect tune. He describes how a motorcycle is put together, how the different parts all have a special place, how a rider can keep that motorcycle functioning well—up over the mountains and down through the valleys and over the desert. What a caring relationship is established between a rider and the motorcycle he loves!

The story is a travel diary. His day-to-day account of the trip is interspersed with a series of reflections about the journey and what it means to him. It is, of course, a symbol of his journey through life—of every man's journey—starting somewhere, ending somewhere. He reflects upon what the journey means and what its purpose is. He loves the riding, just the riding. Trying to describe that deep sense of satisfaction in the riding when everything is all right with the person behind him, he says: "Sometimes it's a little better to travel than to arrive." In urging us, therefore, to accept the reality of the present and to take it all in just as much as we are able to, he comments, "When you want to hurry something, that means that you no longer care about it and you want to get on with other things." He talks about caring right now for what you are doing right now. Spend your energy on the present; don't agonize about tomorrow's goal; those goals don't come. The goal is in the riding, the present.

Caring is everything. That means, among other things, caring for your motorcycle. If you are going to ride it and enjoy it, you naturally take care of it. Persig uses the motorcycle as the symbol of modern technological society. It is the end product of Greek and Roman thought and Western culture. Reason has emerged as the dominant force in our society, and its handmaiden is science. It is the "scientific" understanding of nature that counts. Science is used to control nature, harness it, exploit it. The symbol of this is the motorcycle, the workings of which can be understood by anybody who can read. Persig describes very clearly how the motorcycle works. (If I had had this book in Lawrenceville, I might have got the motorcycle started again myself.)

So if you apply your reason to the motorcycle with care, it will work perfectly. The tune-up makes the motorcycle "hum" when you have made the right adjustments. And when the motorcycle "hums," you "hum." That is, you have done a quality job not only on the motorcycle but on yourself. That, Persig says, is what happens when reason is in control and functions properly. Rational man seeks to do a quality job because he cares. This is true whether he cares for motorcycles or ideas or whatever. The point is that reason and science, caring and quality, all belong together in our Western society and here is the symbol in the cared-for motorcycle.

The theme of the book is that man's nature is most fully expressed when this rational nature—the motorcycle—is joined with his intuitive nature, his feeling, his love nature. The symbol for this is the father's relationship with his son on the back seat. The caring he has for his son, the caring and love he has for his journey and for the motorcycle, are somehow meant to be all of a piece. And this intuitive feeling, this emotional side, joined together with the rational side, makes the whole person. The two natures are two aspects of the same thing. A person who cares about what he sees and does is bound to be a person of quality.

Do you want to live a life of quality? Then care. *Caring* and *quality* emerge as the marks of a whole person. Finally, this is what the book is about. "The real cycle you're working on," he writes, "is a cycle called yourself. The machine that appears to be 'out there' and the person who appears to be 'in here' are not two separate things. They grow toward quality or fall away from quality, together."

I have taken the time to describe this book at such length, not only to suggest that you read it (if you are interested in the world of ideas, you will be fascinated by it), but also because it seems to me to present in nonreligious terms precisely what the Christian Faith is about. It describes a journey, outward and inward, where caring and quality are the essential ingredients. The biblical words are love and truth—lived most fully by Jesus, who was filled with love and truth and who said: I am the Way and the Truth. The goal is a life lived truthfully and lovingly, a life lived now. We are not to worry or drive desperately toward the end of the journey; the end and the way are the same. Our journey is meant to be as satisfying and whole as possible. We are meant to reflect our whole nature in that journey; our emotional as well as our rational nature. Our head and our heart are meant to go together; the songs that we sing with our hearts are meant to make sense to our heads, as we care for one another and for ourselves.

The real cycle we are always working on is ourselves, and as we journey, caring, we always grow toward quality, toward Christ. As we grow toward him on our journey, we remember that he is the Way. It is not simply *our* journey we are taking, it is *his* as well. It's his right now. He won't let us fall off, because his hands are on the handle bars and the cycle he is working on is ourselves, caring for us that we may care and so become quality people—sheer quality, wholly ourselves in love and in Truth.

Jesus—

We can't keep our balance
    without you.
We can't go anywhere,
    be anybody
    without you.

So you be our guide now
    on our journey.
You drive.

Let us rejoice in just the
    day we have,
    as we set out once
    more for this day's
    journey.

Let us rejoice in everything
    and everyone
    just as they are,
    caring for them as you
    do, and loving ourselves
    as you do.

Help us be whole persons
    growing toward holiness
And the safe journey's end
    in you.

7

Being at one with oneself

If you have ever had a sense of the majesty and glory of God, the attraction and loveliness of Christ, or of the power and the joy that surges through you when you are touched by a spirit that you have to call holy, then you have probably felt a deepened sense of unity within yourself. Through such experiences—or even glimmers of such experiences—you become more of a person, more grounded, more centered, less dispersed, less frivolous, held more in one piece.

Curiously, this does not seem to happen if you concentrate upon trying to unify yourself, "to get yourself together," as we say. It comes rather as a by-product, an afterword. Some thing or some force or some experience seems to overwhelm you, to come upon you, to pull you out of yourself, to lift you. In being drawn beyond yourself, you find yourself more at one with yourself.

St. Paul said of Christ, "He is before all things and in him all things hold together." (Col. 1:17)

On the face of it, this seems like an excessive claim. As

we observe the world, there is no overwhelming evidence that this is true. In fact, it might be easier, more obvious, to say that things seem to be falling apart. Societies seem to be static or disintegrating; nations and races and classes seem to be divided, opposed to each other in conflict. It is certainly true on the personal level that many people are so fragile that they seem on the verge of flying apart at any time. Most of us can identify with the man who commented: "Any day that I simply get through, I count as a great victory. If I have survived, I have won."

So just picking up the pieces, trying to put them together into a package that represents some kind of totality, seems almost impossible. The paper that we use for wrapping is torn; the string that we tie things up with gets broken; insides begin to move around and fall out and we have to lean down and pick them up and try to put them all back together again.

The rage we thought we had got over once and for all suddenly swells up and overcomes us, inexplicably triggered. A grief we thought we had come to terms with years ago suddenly floods all over us again. Fears take hold of us in a strange way, and when we try to work them through, we discover they are rooted back in a bereavement or a hostility that we have never really been able to come to terms with. A loose end is destroying us; or a sin that we put behind us as forgiven—and we thought forgotten—suddenly wakes us up in the middle of the night. Maybe we are forgiven, but we have not forgotten. Its power to trouble us is still there. The shadows we thought we had laid to rest rise again. Demons we had driven out sneak back in. Moods we thought we had outgrown with adolescence come back stronger than ever. Slights that we had said we were going to rise above turn out to have a tenacious grip on us.

Life does not lend itself to neat packaging. An apparently strong character reveals weakness underneath; a powerful person is struck down by sickness, his life is in fragments. Great love is expressed, sometimes laced with hate. Compassion and caring are mixed with self-pity and self-loathing. We show courage in facing great crises, and cowardice in facing the picayune challenge of everydayness. Everyday frustrations, irritations, and petty little failures defeat us. Every once in a while we are more noble, more generous, more sacrificing than we had ever thought possible. At times we are so exuberant, we could jump over the moon; at other times we are barely able to drag one foot after another. Bouncing and buoyant one day, we are chastened and chagrined the next.

We cannot seem to get centered, or we try to get our center in something that does not endure. When we are growing up, we tend to concentrate our attention and put our heart's desire upon being accepted by our contemporaries, our peer group. That seems to be the most important thing in our lives. When we enter a room, the question is, "Am I going to be accepted or am I going to be rejected? What can I do to be accepted? How can I help people see that I am an acceptable person, especially when I feel that I am not really acceptable. Will I make it? Will I be popular?" Later in life we create other centers: professional success or business success or personal success, credit ratings, a center in another person or persons, a center in a family. "I am going to live for my family; I am going to be the best mother (or father) that ever was." Such centers, while providing direction and purpose at certain times, never finally unify because they themselves, by themselves, cannot endure. We put too much of a burden upon another person when we say, "My life is going to be fulfilled in you." It is too much for a marriage to hold, too much for a family to hold. We put our fulfillment, our center, in the health of the relationship to which we belong. We have set our hearts on something or someone. We have fulfilled our heart's desires and those desires have turned into ashes. We are still not satisfied. There is a deeper and deeper longing for a center. It is hard to find. The immortal and the eternal can never be wholly incorporated within or identified with the mortal and the temporal. However important mortal persons and temporal values may be, they cannot be the center.

Paul faced up to the war within himself as he sought to determine his center, and asked himself, "Who will deliver me from this body of death?" He quickly responded, "Thanks be to God through Jesus Christ our Lord. . . . There is . . . no condemnation for those who are in Christ Jesus."

That doesn't seem to be much of an answer, but it really is. Paul was saying that the ambiguities, contradictions, and conflicts of life were so powerful that all he could do was refer the whole mixed bag to Christ and say, in effect: "Look, it is yours. You take it. I thank you for it." Christ became his center. "This body, this love, this hate, this will, all mixed up, divided, distorted—it's all me, and it's all *yours. You* take it. *You* do something with it. *You* renew it. *You* pull it together. Christ, you are my center."

What he could not do for himself, what none of us can do for ourselves, Paul said Christ can do. "All things (including me), he says, are held together in Him." We can put our center there in him, if we decide to do so; that is if we decide to trust him. Not perfectly. There are always untied ends hanging out, but most of our lives are held together in a unifying spirit.

Another way of putting this is to say that, as you discern the spirit of your true self rising within you, you *trust* it. You let that center, that spirit which rises from the center within you, that self within you, draw you into a more whole self. Let that spirit draw to the light your shadowed side. Don't try to keep your shadowed side down or to hide it. Trust that as it is lifted to the light it will be incorporated into the light. Your hostilities and rages can be incorporated into that true self which is the light that lightens every man who comes into the world. That is the Christ-light within you drawing you. *Let* him draw you. Then things fall into place. Do not *you* try; let *him* try. Let him draw you into more and more wholeness, more you.

All things in life are held together by him. All things you remember of the past that plague you; all those things of the past that you carried into this day; all circumstances and failures, sins and tragedies and griefs, all victories and joys and hopes—are held together in him. You become increasingly a whole person as you let your past fill into the present, and then look forward. You become increasingly one person because you are increasingly becoming one in him. He renews. He draws. He heals. He makes whole.

Finally, however difficult it may seem, however incredible it may seem (and it is incredible), you can also be at one in the spirit with everyone, those you love most and those you love least, those you care for and those you do not care about at all. You can give them over to Christ in the spirit, just as you give yourself in the spirit. You can wish them well in the spirit; even when you are in violent disagreement with them, you can wish them well. You can hold them before God in the spirit. You can be at one with everyone in the spirit because it is the spirit of Christ. He is drawing all men.

We participate in his work as we give others over to him. Excluding people from the spirit brings division; including them brings wholeness. In him, separations, enmities, divisions begin to fade away. So let your varied, distinct, diverse, scattered loves be held together in him.

Let him draw those separated from you to himself in the
spirit. Offer them to him. Keep the focus on him. Let him
do the drawing. He said he would. He does. Let him draw
you, and all things, all manner of things, shall be well in
him.

> Gentle Jesus, press
>   us with your presence.
>
> Draw us with your grace
>   and gentleness.
> Treat those
>   for whom we pray
>   —gently, gracefully,
>   eternally.
>
> With them we are
>   one in the spirit
> as we are in you
>   drawing us
> holding all things together
>   in this life
> and in the world to come.

8

God's question to you

Christ be with me, Christ within me,
Christ behind me, Christ before me,
Christ beside me, Christ to win me,
Christ to comfort and restore me,
Christ beneath me, Christ above me,
Christ in quiet, Christ in danger,
Christ in hearts of all that love me,
Christ in mouth of friend and stranger.

ST. PATRICK[5]

Christ in everything. God in everything. Christ in everyone. God in everyone. In whatever we are in, Christ in, God in. In whatever happens to us, Christ happening. In however we respond, Christ responding. The one with whom we are dealing in all the events of life, without and within, is a "You." "You—Christ." "You—God." "You—the Spirit."

Lest the impression be given that this is an interesting

point of view from a very primitive saint who went to a
pagan land to drive the snakes out and to establish a
Christian society amongst a pagan people, let me now
quote a contemporary saint who is also a statesman.

In 1958, when Dag Hammarskjöld was Secretary Gen-
eral of the United Nations, he wrote in his diary:

. . . you are *one* in God, and
God is wholly in you,
just as, for you, He is wholly in all you meet.
With this faith, in prayer you descend into yourself to meet the
     Other,
in the steadfastness and light of this union,
see that all things stand, like yourself, alone before God. . . .

In the faith which is "God's marriage to the soul," *everything*,
     therefore, has a meaning.
So live, then, that you may use what has been put into your
     hand. . . .[6]

Both St. Patrick and Dag Hammarskjöld say the same
thing. "Do not try," they say, "to distinguish too sharply
between yourself and the selves of others and God's
self" . . . "You are one in God and God is wholly in you,
just as he is wholly in all you meet"—"Christ be with me,
Christ within me, Christ in hearts of all that love me,
Christ in mouth of friend and stranger."

You descend into your self and there in that inner self
you meet another Self. There deep responds to deep.
Spirit responds to spirit. You may say, God responds to
God and you participate in that process. Or you may say,
Man responds to man and God participates in that
process. Either way, God and man work, merge, together.

You can speak of our life in God or God's life in us.
When we affirm our selfhood, we are affirming God's
selfhood. When we are making God great, we are making
ourselves great. We are somebodies because we are God's
body. We are in him, and he is in us. We do not need,

therefore, to try to separate too sharply our self, others' selves, and God's self. The more we accept of our self, the more we accept of other selves, the more we accept God's self.

Hammarskjöld says that because we are one in God, *everything* has a meaning. Everything—death as well as life. There is no meaning in death unless there is a meaning in life, and no meaning in life unless there is a meaning in death. There is meaning in betrayal as well as in loyalty. A relationship that is broken has meaning as well as a relationship that stays together. *Everything* has meaning: pain as well as joy; suffering as well as health; evil as well as good; yearning as well as fulfillment; the loss of life just as much as being filled to overflowing; hate as well as love.

These things are not the same. They are different, but they are bound together and in that binding together *everything* has a meaning. "So live then," he concludes, "that you may use what has been put into your hand."

So there has been put into your hand this day, all that is good in your life, all that is bad, all the breaking and all the holding, all the depths and all the heights. Whatever mixture there is in your life right now has a meaning. You do not have to change anything. You have only to take your life at this moment as from him, and to respond to him in everything, in every person. And to say as you respond, "You—Christ," "You—God," "You—Spirit."

If Christ is there "within you," "in friend and stranger," in *everything*, do you want him there? Do you *really* want him there? Yes or no?

The Lord knows there is good reason to say No. We all say No at times. I would like to keep Christ at a distance. I am very uncomfortable if he comes too close. I like him over there in that Bible story because it is all written down and I can open it when I want to read about it and close it when I don't. He is there in a book.

Or we put him in a church. We can walk by the church and not go in. He is there and we are safe from him.

Or we put him in some sacraments. If we put him in sacraments, then we can lock him up in a box, put him away, and open the box once in a while and greet him; then close the box again.

Or we put him with the clergy. He is their line of business. Let them take care of Christ for us. That is what they can offer us. So if the body of Christ is to do anything, let the clergy do it. They made the choice to lead a professional religious life. It serves them right.

We can put him anywhere we can be safe from him, where he does not press too hard, but where we can call on him when we need him. But, we say, I would lose my own integrity if I let him come on too strong in my life. Then he would be making decisions. If I am a free, mature human being, I have to make them myself. I cannot give up control. I want to be a strong person. I cannot let him get involved in everything I am involved in—that's too much. No, I do not want him on such intimate personal terms.

That is a natural, understandable response. I believe Christ respects that. He will wait. He has plenty of time. We do not like being second choice, but he does not even mind being last choice. So if you say No, he will wait.

But if you should say, "Yes, I *do* want him here within me and within those I am working with, in every activity of my life" then that response to him is to participate in his response to life. It is to say Yes to life—just as it is. Yes. Not Yes when things get straightened out, but Yes right now. Yes to everybody who is already involved in your life just the way they are. To say Yes is not simply to find Christ—it is to express him, right now.

There are only two answers: Yes or No. Any decision to wait until later is, in fact, to say No. The inability to make up our minds because all of the evidence has not come in is to say No. To say I am not sure is to say No. To say I do not know whether I really want him or not is to say No. These are all perfectly understandable reasons for saying No.

But God, through our No, may be preparing us to say Yes. The best reason for saying No is that you do not believe God exists. You did once, but you don't now. He did not measure up in the experiences of your life. Or your ideas of God did not measure up. They were not capable of dealing with the abrasions in life. You could not face them and believe in God at the same time. Or, perhaps the people you knew who believed in him did not measure up. They belonged to the Church but it did not mean a thing. You knew it and they knew it.

For whatever reason, you have come to the time when you believe nothing. Nothing. No point in anything. In your worst moments you might say, I've tried everything and nothing works. There's no point in God or people or society or money or marriage or success or alcohol or adultery—or anything. When that time comes and everything is stripped away, the question remains, "What do you want to do? What do *you* want to do?" When there is nothing, this is the question. It is God's question.

How can it be God's question, you may ask, when I don't believe in God? Make it life's question then. It is a question that presses in on you just because you are living. How are you going to respond to life? With a Yes or a No? How are you going to respond to the lives around you? With a Yes or a No?

God bestows great dignity upon us when he asks us such a question and does not coerce us to answer his way. When we say Yes to life, to others, and to ourselves, not because we *have* to but because we *want* to, we are in fact saying Yes to God. We are responding as mature men and women in that perfect freedom God gives us. We are responding not to power, but to love. We choose him because that is our heart's desire. That is love choosing love.

He is asking us to stand on our own feet, make our own choice, decide for ourselves. It is as if he said, "Look, this relationship is a partnership. You have to take your part. You're grown up now. Trust yourself. Trust your deepest self. That is where I am. That is where my spirit and yours meet and touch each other. So trust yourself for my sake. Do what you want to do. Try to do it for love's sake—for others. That is the way my will is done. When you trust yourself in love, that is trusting me."

Of course, we are prepared for some of our ego to die so that our true self may live. Insofar as we are willing not to have our own way, we set other people's selves free. Through dying to self we enter upon successive new levels of deeper selves being revealed with power.

In the life, death, and resurrection of Christ we see the mighty love of God enacted—the same love which is our true self, God's self in us. It is not a spooky faraway thing; it is his life in you and me right now.

In the light of that light within and in the light of the cross which shines from Calvary, we take up our journey and walk with him. And the first step is right now.

Christ be with me, Christ within me,
Christ behind me, Christ before me,
Christ beside me, Christ to win me,
Christ to comfort and restore me,
Christ beneath me, Christ above me,
Christ in quiet, Christ in danger,
Christ in hearts of all that love me,
Christ in mouth of friend and stranger.

9

Zapped by Jesus

The TV series "Religious America" included a visit to a Pentecostal church in Los Angeles. Toward the end of the service individual members of the congregation were invited to come forward in what is traditionally known as the "altar call." They stood before the minister, who said a prayer, lifted his hand over them, and sometimes touched them. They immediately fell backwards in a swoon and were caught by ushers and stretched out on the floor. They had been—in the words of the minister as he explained it later—"zapped by Jesus."

There are experiences that people go through that are so intense that a change of direction takes place in their lives. They know tomorrow can never be exactly the same as yesterday. Something happens of such intensity that a milestone is marked, and the person sets off in a new direction, possessed by a conviction that comes, sometimes quietly like a thief in the night, at other times like the blinding sun at noonday, but always with a startling force. Such a person becomes a new person, or at least a different one. Paul's experience on the Damascus road (Acts 26:9-23) is a classic description of this conversion experience. He was turned from a persecutor of the Christians into the pre-eminent Christian of the early Church, ultimately a martyr to persecution himself. He changed from persecutor to follower because he had been "zapped" by Jesus.

Whoever makes a decision to turn his life toward Jesus, to recognize him as the Lord, has somewhere—either in one dramatic experience or in a series of quiet undramatic ones—been turned by some spirit that has broken through into the core of his being. All of a sudden, things fall into place.

Discoveries in science are frequently like that—a breaking through into the consciousness of the scientist when he has been thinking about something else. Artists often say that they are possessed when they paint or compose, or when they sing. The Muse is referred to as being present to writers, or sometimes, as they say, "the Muse has vanished." A person who is inspired to become himself on a more intense level may say, "It was as though I were on cloud nine" or "It was like coming off a high" or "I was really inspired." "I was in the spirit and I knew, with all my being, exactly what I had to do."

The things that prepare a person for such an experience are an important part of the event itself. What goes before creates the context out of which experiences arise. You work very hard on a problem, or you wrestle with a question that you know you somehow have got to answer; and there is no answer. Then one day you wake up in the morning and the answer is there. Some people proclaim that experiences of such an intense nature can be brought on by drugs or alcohol. It is certainly true that drugs and alcohol do bring dreams and visions (sometimes D.T.'s), but it is doubtful that the deliberate distortion of normal consciousness ever makes it possible to take positive steps toward creativity. The experiences of a "high" at night are usually a nightmare the next morning, or a hangover.

Others affirm that these experiences do not need artificial stimulation but can be brought on by meditation, bodily discipline, or proper breathing. Sometimes nature itself—the water, the wind, the stars—can trigger "minor ecstasies." In our culture today there are many purveyors of spiritual experience who guarantee that you will be "turned on" spiritually if you follow their technique—and usually pay their fees. Just as there are purveyors of the flesh, so there are purveyors of the spirit, and they both have one thing in common: the experience, either in the flesh or in the spirit, is an end in itself. The experience itself is worthwhile regardless of its consequences.

No Christian spiritual experience is an end in itself. No spiritual experience by itself is necessarily good. Whether it is good or not depends upon what happens afterwards. What is significant about inspiration is not that you are inspired, but that you make certain decisions differently than you did before. There is nothing more significant about exaltation in itself than there is in depression in itself. When you are exalted, what follows? It is what develops out of exaltation and depression that is important. How can you tell whether your ecstasy is Jesus or the Devil zapping you? How do you determine whether your intense emotional experiences are divine or demonic?

Let me suggest three criteria:

First, if Jesus is zapping you, you become more responsible in the network of relationships you already have, more moral, more sensitive to the ethical dimensions of the network where you are. Jesus zaps you by turning you outward to be faithful to the obligations you already have. When you have an intense emotional experience and come out of it saying "the hell with everything," you can be certain it is not Jesus calling you to that way of life. A vision to leave your wife and children, or husband and children, or to leave your job, or forget your debts, or take off, is a vision all right, but it is from the Devil, not from Jesus. The way life is held together most of the time is by going about your business quietly, not letting down the people for whom you are responsible.

Second, when Jesus zaps you, there is always a clarification of yourself. You become more unified, more whole, less fragmented, more integrated, more the same outside as inside. What you appear to be is really what you are. There is less division, less pretense, less phoniness. Sometimes you are purged by these experiences. The nonessentials drop away. The frantic desires for more and more and more drop away. You become a less cluttered person—in the best sense of the word, a simple person.

That may mean that you will have to give up some things, sacrifice some goals, renounce some habits. You may even, for Jesus' sake, have to give up people who in other circumstances would be perfectly appropriate to have. To be in touch with Jesus and to be in touch with his spirit, you sometimes have to give up possessing, owning, and touching other things and people. That is called sacrifice. If it is a loving sacrifice that you make— or if you want it to be a loving sacrifice—you can be certain it is Jesus who is zapping you.

Finally, you have a sense that you no longer have to be in charge of yourself. God is. He is poking around everywhere in your life so that he might draw you to him. Sometimes through some experiences he pokes so hard that you *know* you have been zapped. You know it is God. You can then turn to love him more securely, and to love all those people who have been given you more freely.

When Jesus zaps you, you become a new person, or at

least begin to become one. When this happens, your love of others turns from possessing them to affirming them, helping them become renewed, more whole. When you are undergirding them, helping them become themselves, they are being zapped, and it is Jesus zapping.

10

This mystery: Christ in you ... the hope of glory

How do you identify the spiritually mature person? Do you consider yourself spiritually mature? Are you an adult in the life of the spirit, or are you immature? Are you standing still? Or are you growing? How do you evaluate yourself?

I am not now referring to religious *knowledge,* although that is important and has its place, but to religious *experience.* It is not knowledge *about* God, but knowledge *of* God that moves people. Do you have any first-hand experience of God? Can you say, "Yes, I know God—and not by hearsay. I know him for myself"?

Can you identify experiences in your own life where you came to some personal knowledge of God? Have you had any people in your life you can point to and say, "through these people, I grew in understanding what life was all about and what God was about"? Most people, perhaps everybody who has any sense of the presence of

God in his life, have come to that understanding because at some time, often as a child, they have had a set of relationships with people who themselves had a sense of that presence of God—a parent, a grandparent, an older friend. Sometimes children get it in church; sometimes they get it from their Godparents, those who spoke in the name of God when the child was named. Have you ever taken the time to identify those people who have in some measure been "God-bearers" for you? It is a superb spiritual exercise to write down their names and to thank God for them. To be able to identify them may help you identify God, so that you can say, "Yes, I know him." Who are those people?

What experiences have you had wherein you have become aware of God? Was it when you came to the end of your rope and you knew that there was no power in yourself to help you move on and you had to turn yourself over to something outside yourself, some power, some God, to get the help you needed? Was it that kind of an experience? Each week thousands of people gather together in meetings of Alcoholics Anonymous because God is helping them stop drinking. They experienced God at the end of their rope. And so can you, when you give yourself to a power beyond yourself and wait expectantly for that power to help you.

Or perhaps you come to the edge of the hospital bed and you look at a person you love, and you know there is nothing further that can be done—no operation, no medicine, no doctor. All has been done that can be done. And you put that person—maybe a child, maybe a mother—into God's hands and you say, "God, she's yours." When God takes over that person—and you *know* it—and you leave her in God's hands and walk away strong because you are content to leave her there, then you have experienced God. So what are your experiences of God? Forgiveness because you have confessed something that has been deeply hidden? Awe because you have been lifted up, inspired? A sense of peace because you have been reconciled? A sense of purpose because you came back to yourself, back into the mainstream of life? Well-being because you were sick from self-indulgence, like the Prodigal Son, and you were healed? Enthusiasm because you had been caught up with a sense of direction for your life? What are the experiences which enable you to say, "I think I have experienced God"?

To be spiritually mature is to have a sense of your own being, to have a sense of your own identity, to know who you are like, what you are like. To say, "That's the kind of person I am; and I'm both glad about it and a little unhappy about it." To be spiritually mature is to be able to identify yourself as *somebody,* and to sense that that *somebody* is affirmed by God. In part, you are who you are because you have recognized and acknowledged that power—a power beyond yourself who is saying Yes to you, affirming you. It is not that God belongs to you; it is to recognize that you belong to God. You discover that you are able to live your life more fully when you put yourself more and more in touch with yourself, your deep-core self, and recognize that self as pressing upon you—that is God.

It is put very simply by Douglas Steere: "The more I pray the better it goes, and the less I pray the worse it goes." If you have had that sense, or anything like it, then you are becoming mature in the spirit; always becoming, never attaining; moving, never resting, never completing the moving. Are you becoming the person you want to become? Are you maturing in the spirit?

The spiritual adult is always growing. He is always moving out. He is always becoming more than he has been. This usually means being drawn into the lives of others—caring, not withdrawing. He may be a private person, but in his innermost being, in his essence, in his own deep spirit, he identifies with other people, or with some other people. He moves into the essence of their being and is able to identify with them in the Spirit. When he identifies with them in the Spirit, he is there to strengthen them, to support them in their understanding of the Spirit. He is never there to remake them, judge them, or reform them in his image; he only wants to help them listen to the Spirit speaking to them and to the words that the Spirit speaks. The more he is able to identify himself with people who are quite unlike himself —the rich with the poor, the healthy with the handicapped, those who have friends with the lonely, those who are well-adjusted with the troubled—the more mature he becomes in the Spirit.

What he trusts is the Spirit and the leading of the Spirit. Therefore, he is open not only to life, people, and to moving away from himself toward them, but he is also open to *mystery*. The more he moves toward the mystery of all life in the Spirit, the more he can appropriate, take into himself, all the experiences of life—the bad as well as the good—and know that somehow in the Spirit they all make sense because they all make up the fabric of life.

To be able to trust that mystery, to be sensitive to the movement of that mystery—the mysterious joys as well as the mysterious tragedies—is to be spiritually mature. The key is the trusting of the Spirit each day, a day at a time, that day only. It is putting your trust in the process of living on the basis of your own experience—nobody else's experience, only yours. You decide. It is your life. Do not look to somebody else to straighten your life out. Do not look to somebody else to give you the meaning of life. Do not look to somebody else to tell you how you should live. Do not look to somebody else to give you the answers to the mystery of life. It is a mystery for everybody. Nobody else can tell you what's what. No one else ever persuades you about your life, its values and meaning. Even if somebody should come back from the dead and tell you, it would not make the slightest difference. It is only the Spirit that can tell you.

You know that Spirit. You know it now. If you are in the Spirit, your values are different. You do not spend your life trying to collect "ribbons"—whether the "ribbons" are first-class breeding, or first-class jobs, or first-class bank accounts. Those do not mean anything eternally. What does mean something eternally is the Spirit you trust, the Spirit that comes to you and dwells within you and rises within you and gladdens your heart as you trust it. It lifts you into a different dimension and existence of living. It gives you a different perspective, a different way of evaluating what is going on about you and what you are participating in.

This spiritual maturity—living in the spirit, trusting the mystery—can be described poetically. William Blake puts it this way:

> He who bends to himself a joy
> Does the winged life destroy;
> But he who kisses the joy as it flies
> Lives in eternity's sunrise.[7]

If you try to bend life, to make it your own, you destroy it. Kiss it, treat it gently, love it—then you are carried by it into the sunrise of eternity. That is the Spirit—living in it—now and always. Indeed that is living eternally now. Eternal life is not simply something after death; eternal life is now, living in the Spirit.

A contemporary poet, Robert Penn Warren, having described how people who have gone from the mystery of living into the mystery of dying still hold a claim upon him, concludes his poem:

> All items above belong in the world
> In which all things are continuous,

And are parts of the original dream which
I am now trying to discover the logic of. This
Is the process whereby the pain of
    the past in its pastness
May be converted into the future tense
Of joy.[8]

That is it. The future tense is joy. So when the Spirit comes into your life, kiss it gently, now, as it flies. "Then the pain of the past in its pastness may be converted into the future tense of joy." The continuity of the process—past, present, and future—is held together by the Spirit, by God, by the One with whom we negotiate life's meanings. This absolute moment now is God. He holds the past and the future together.

The mystery that has baffled thoughtful, sensitive people from the beginning of time has been made clear for Christian people: It is that, in those who recognize the Spirit and trust it, God lives. The Spirit that you are sensitive to within is God himself. The quality of life in the people who have helped you to know God is God. The prayer that you offer by the bedside is God. When you know who you are because you know you are God's, you know God. The meaning of the mystery is in your life—in God in your life.

The last word on Spiritual maturity, trusting the Spirit in the mystery of existence, is St. Paul's:

The mystery hidden for ages and generations is now made manifest. . . . How great . . . are the riches of the glory of this mystery, which is Christ in you, the hope of glory.

Colossians 1:27

To grow in the Spirit, to grow in joy, to become more and more uniquely yourself trusting the Spirit in the mystery of life is to grow in Christ in you—*experiencing* him, the hope of glory.

PART II

In Death

*An Interior Drama
in Seven Scenes*

Prologue:
Contemporary man looks
at the cross

So, Pilate, wishing to satisfy the crowd, released for them Barabbas; and having scourged Jesus, he delivered him to be crucified.

And the soldiers led him away inside the palace (that is, the praetorium); and they called together the whole battalion. And they clothed him in a purple cloak, and plaiting a crown of thorns they put it on him. And they began to salute him, "Hail, King of the Jews!" And they struck his head with a reed, and spat upon him, and they knelt down in homage to him. And when they had mocked him, they stripped him of the purple cloak, and put his own clothes on him. And they led him out to crucify him.

MARK 15:15-20

The stage is a church. The congregation gathers, settles, looks at a large crucifix placed in the middle of the chancel. It is noon of Good Friday. Into the church wanders a middle-aged man, John Everyman, the Contemporary Man. He takes his place, settles down, looks at the crucifix.

John has a wife, Jane, and three teen-age children: two boys, one girl. Jane is a typical suburban housewife with special interest in art and has a part-time job at the local museum. Theirs is an average middle-class American family.

John works in New York (or Boston or Chicago or San Francisco) and they live in Darien (or Chestnut Hill or Lake Forest or Marin County). He is a college graduate and vice-president of his insurance company. He takes the 7:45 train to work every morning, and the 5:28 back every night. He stands in the same place on the platform every morning, sits in the same seat in the train, and reads the same paper. In the evening, he usually does not get a seat until he is halfway home.

John works hard—too hard—and he often takes work home with him. He does not see much of his family, and seldom relaxes enough to have a good time with them. He sometimes feels he is being driven. On Friday and Saturday nights he may drink too many martinis. He has a good income, and spends it all. In twelve more years he will own his house. He is a "white Anglo-Saxon Protestant," was baptized as a child, and is a nominal member of a church. He drives the younger children to Church School each Sunday and returns home to read the paper. His wife goes to church on special occasions.

This does not mean that John has no religion. He has. It's the Golden Rule. He just has no use for "organized religion." He is a decent fellow, would like to love his neighbor as he does himself, but has seldom wondered why he doesn't. He has little idea about the Cross, why Christ died on it, and he suspects there must be more to it than meets the eye. More than once he has promised himself that one day he would sit down and try to figure it out. This is the day.

Early in the afternoon his last appointment for the day was cancelled and he was able to leave the office sooner than usual. On his way to the station he passed a church with a sign: *Three Hour Service—Good Friday*. What he remembered most about Good Friday from his childhood was hot cross buns.

So he stopped in. "I think I'll keep that promise to myself," he said. At least I'll get some quiet, a chance to think. And tonight over cocktails, I'll say to Jane, "I'll bet you can't guess where I've been for three hours this afternoon." She'll say, "To the movies." And I'll say, "To church. What do you think of that?"

So the Contemporary Man has come to the church. He has come to a resting place in his life. Before the cross. On the cross is another Man. John is going to look at him, think about him, talk to him.

> *And when they came to a place called Golgotha (which means the place of the skull), they offered him wine to drink, mingled with gall; but when he tasted it, he would not drink it. And when they had crucified him, they divided his garments among them by casting lots; then they sat down and kept watch over him there.*
>
> MATTHEW 27:33-36

Scene I:
Anxiety, guilt and
the psychiatrist

*And when they came to the place which is called
The Skull, there they crucified him, and the crimi-
nals, one on the right and one on the left.
And Jesus said, "Father, forgive them; for they
know not what they do."*

LUKE 23:33-34

The damndest thing happens when you suddenly
come in out of a dizzy, hectic schedule and sit down,
plunk, and try to compose yourself and be quiet. It's
pretty hard to slow down—just like that. You try to pull
yourself together. Though your body may sit still, your
heart keeps on pounding away, thoughts keep whirling
through your mind. Your brain doesn't slow down at all.

In fact, it seems to speed up. New thoughts seem to pile up—thoughts you never knew you had. It's as though they had been lurking down there in the depths somewhere just waiting for a chance to surface. You sit down, try to be quiet, and—whammo!—there they are racing all over the place.

Talk about fantasy. You don't need any drugs to go on a trip. All you need is to let these weird fantasies take hold. Those dreams that are so bizarre you hardly think you could have them. Yet there they are. *Your* dreams. Nobody else's. And if you are in them having all these fantastic experiences—frightening, fascinating—it's because you put yourself there. Nobody else puts you into your dreams. You are there because they are part of your nature, part of you. If you go off the deep end in your dreams, it's because you want to. If you go off with somebody, it's because you want to. If suddenly you are frightened, it's because there is something down deep to be frightened of. If you wake up in a cold sweat feeling guilty, it's because you *are* guilty—of something.

Maybe that is why I keep working so hard. When I keep working long enough and hard enough, I am so exhausted when I get home at night that when I try to slow down I go right off to sleep—especially if I have a nightcap or two. Then I don't have to worry about what is really at the bottom of my heart. If I am exhausted enough, I don't have to worry about the thoughts and fears and anxieties that I carry around with me all the time, apparently.

I guess this is what the psychiatrist meant last summer when he told me that this was a compulsive neurosis. "The trouble with you," he said, "and with most people who lead your kind of life, is that you have a neurosis that makes it impossible for you to slow down. That's why you have heart attacks and high blood pressure and ulcers. You are just driven, and you let yourself be driven. You like to be driven, because then you don't have to face yourself."

Well, maybe he's right. It was strange how I got mixed up with that psychiatrist in the first place. Everything really began to break and crumble and unfold in my mind that Fourth of July weekend last summer. What a hot weekend that was! I had to come back from the shore every day to spend two hours in the office with the auditor. The rest of the time I was free. I was never so lonely in all my life. There was nothing to do. Everybody was out of town.

I had lots of time to think. It was really the first time in my life I had so much time to think. But it didn't seem to help, because I had to think all by myself. I was all alone. Soon I began to get uneasy, almost frightened with the thoughts I had. For the first time, no matter how much I drank at night I couldn't get to sleep. I'd go to bed exhausted. I'd wake up exhausted. I was keyed up. There wasn't anybody I could talk to. As a matter of fact, I always had been kind of keyed up—uptight. I'd always been sort of frightened and anxious about the way things might turn out. It seemed to me one night last summer that all of these little anxieties and fears suddenly began to become a hard, tight ball inside of me, getting bigger and bigger, and I was afraid I was going to burst with it. I knew I had to do something, so I went to a psychiatrist.

Once I made up my mind that I needed one, wanted one, it was easy enough to do. I just asked my doctor to recommend one, saying it was for a friend of mine. I must have had this in the back of my mind for a long time. I didn't have to be crazy to go. I just knew I couldn't cope all by myself the way things were going. I saw him three times a week for three months. He was helpful, pointed out a few things and I began to feel easier.

He told me that almost everybody was uptight inside. Almost everybody was a little frightened. What are we frightened about? "Everybody is anxious," he said. "Everybody is a little scared of everybody else. Some people are frightened just because they are alive." Why is that? I wondered.

There was another thing he said that struck me because I had suspected it all my life long, but I thought I was the only one who felt this way. He said nearly everybody feels guilty at one time or another. I had felt guilty for as long as I could remember. Then he said that most people don't know what they're guilty of. Well, that was me all right. I didn't know what I'd been guilty of. Oh, I had done lots of things I was ashamed of, but the guilt I was carrying around was all out of proportion to them. This was something different. "It's like people going around frightened of each other," he said. "They look at each other and they all know they are guilty; they all want to be forgiven but they don't know what they want to be forgiven for."

I knew what he meant. Every once in a while I would wake up because I'd been having a bad dream. In the dream I had always broken the law. I'd stolen some money or murdered somebody and I was going to be found out. Or I had committed a sin that no one knew about. Anyway, in the dream I knew I was guilty but it was hard to pin down what the guilt was about. Then when I woke up I had that great sense of relief, knowing it was only a dream. Yet I wonder why I still knew I was guilty—of something.

"You know, as a psychiatrist I am really just a sponge for people," he told me one day. "I let them come in and tell me how frightened they are. They feel a lot better because there is someone to listen to them. Then I let them tell me what it is they think they are guilty of. They go as far as they can and I say, 'Yes.' I soak up this poison in people's systems and, at least for a while, that is a part of the burden they don't have to carry any longer."

Well, in the course of these three months I told him everything I could think of. It wasn't like going to confession exactly, though it was partly like that. I just got rid of a lot of garbage I'd been carrying around inside me for years. I told him how I felt about my parents, what I did in the army, and how I felt about my wife and the kids and the job and my boss. As I listened to myself, I thought, "Gosh, it's not all that bad! I'm not such a bad fellow. I'm pretty responsible. I carry my share." How come, then, I'm still a little frightened, still have those tremors of anxiety down inside, still feel kind of guilty? How can I feel guilty when I haven't really done much wrong—at least not recently?

Anyway, these fears keep rising. This guilt seems to come from a source much deeper than any level where I've been able to think, much deeper than just identifying what I've done that I ought not to have done. Sometimes it seems as though I were let down (and maybe everybody is) into a great big ocean. There is nothing around me except icy fear and guilt. Most of the time, I have to struggle to keep my head above the water so I don't drown in it. It's too big a problem for that psychiatrist. It goes much deeper into the very business of who I am and why I'm here, why a relatively decent fellow like me should get so confused and bewildered and tripped up.

So, since I am here in front of this cross with myself and my life and you, I am going to try to figure out what, if anything, you've got to say to me. Maybe my trouble is I should have been in here long ago. Maybe I've been too far away. But anyhow, I'm here. Perhaps if I just sit and look at you, you may be the one who can do something about this fear and guilt. Wouldn't it be something if you could? Do you suppose you could ever make me innocent as a baby again, Jesus, as innocent as I once must have been? Do you suppose you could really ever make me clean? My trouble is that I'm not clean. Maybe that's the reason I'm afraid. Maybe what you can do for me is something nobody else can do—let me know that finally there isn't anything to be afraid of. (Or is there?)

Maybe my problem is just "being." What is it then that makes me guilty? What makes me afraid? Can you do something about that guilt? What were those words you just said on the cross. "Father, forgive them for they know not what they do." Forgive whom? Those fellows who put you there? For what? Because they don't know what they did? Well, that's me, Jesus. I don't know what I've done, but I do know that I need to be forgiven. I don't know why I'm afraid, but I know that I am. Is that why you are here? Is this why I happened to come in this afternoon to hear you say, "Father, forgive him"?

I remember a phrase from Sunday School: "Make me a clean heart, O God, and renew a right spirit within me." That's what I need, Jesus—a clean heart and a right spirit. I can't make it, but maybe you can, Jesus. Jesus, can you hear me?

Scene II:
The man who is always out to lunch

> One of the criminals who were hanged railed at him, saying, "Are you not the Christ? Save yourself and us!"
> But the other rebuked him, saying, "Do you not fear God, since you are under the same sentence of condemnation?
> And we indeed justly; for we are receiving the due reward of our deeds; but this man has done nothing wrong."
> And he said, "Jesus, remember me when you come in your kingly power."
> And he said to him, "Truly, I say to you, today you will be with me in Paradise."

LUKE 23:39-43

You know, Jesus, just sitting here and looking at the cross it suddenly occurred to me that I might be better off outside. I could have taken the time to call on Jones when that other appointment was cancelled. I might have had a chance to see him this afternoon. Except that if I had called him, his secretary would probably have answered the phone and said, "Oh, I'm sorry, Mr. Jones is out to lunch." I call him at eleven o'clock in the morning and I call him at three o'clock in the afternoon, and for the past two months the answer is always the same: "I'm sorry, Mr. Jones is out to lunch." It's very frustrating, you know, Jesus, when you try to get in touch with somebody and you can never reach him. It's very annoying when you have an assignment to see a man and he's always out. It's very difficult to try to touch somebody when he's never quite there. I'm beginning to wonder if there really is a Jones.

I suppose that's the reason for the phrase people use to describe somebody that they don't like. They say, "He's out to lunch." It used to be "He's a meatball!" You couldn't touch him. Now "He's out to lunch" or "He's out" or even "He's lunchy." That's a distinctive phrase to describe somebody you can never quite touch. It's a devastating experience to be known as "out to lunch." I suppose that's what I was most concerned about when I was young. I suppose that's what most young people are concerned about—are they "in" or "out"? Are they accepted or not accepted?

But it's not just an adolescent problem. As I think about it, it seems I spend a good deal of my time trying to persuade people that I'm not the kind of fellow who's "out to lunch," that I am a pretty good guy, that I'm worthy of their acceptance. If they are wise, they would see that I was really "in" and they would let me "in." That's why we teach these little tricks to salesmen.

Always ask after the other fellow's health first. Always say, "How's your wife?" "How are your children?" It's even better if you remember their names. Make them think that you are really interested in them. I want them to think I am interested in them in order that they will think I am really a pretty good fellow. I wonder if they do? I wonder how many of them honestly think down deep inside that I'm with them. Or whether they say, "That fellow John, that insurance man, he's out to lunch." Those people have never really met me as a person.

I've never had thoughts like this before, Jesus. But this is one of the things that I suppose happens when you come in and sit down and you know you are not going to do a thing for three hours. When you've simmered down enough to put some honest thought on it, it's probably true that I *am* "out to lunch" to most people. There are not many people outside my family (or inside, for that matter) who really know me. There are not many people who know me the way I think I know myself down deep inside, the way I honestly am: my wife, once in a while; my parents, almost never; my children, off and on. Wouldn't it be just great if there were somebody?

Well, as far as that goes, there aren't many people I really know either. I've got enough acquaintances, neighbors, people we play bridge or golf with, go to parties with. But not many of these people are people I would really lay it on the line with and unburden myself the way I'm unburdening myself to you, Jesus. There's probably not one of them I would want to let know what's going on in my mind right now. Not many people I could ever talk to. My college roommate, maybe, if we could go back thirty years. I don't suppose I ever talked to anybody like this since I was a little boy, except that psychiatrist, who got paid for it.

How come this is the way it works out, Jesus? Here I am half way through life and there's hardly anyone who knows me the way I am. The closest friends I've had I made years ago. Only two or three friends since the war. How come? Here I am in this mature age, surrounded by perfectly decent people at home and in the office. I've played with them, worked with them. I'm with these people all day long, and yet not one of them is close enough for me to level with. It's a strange thing, Jesus, but I'll bet that if all these people in this church right now were talking to you the way I am, they'd say pretty much the same thing: that they do not have people around them who really know them the way they believe they are.

John Donne says: "No man is an island." What a silly statement! The trouble is *every* man is an island. Every man, isolated, alone, surrounded by lots of other islands, but in between them, water. It comes and it goes. Sometimes we can walk across when it's low tide, but most of the time, we can't even touch hands. We try to throw a line, we pull somebody over. Maybe he stays for a time, but he always goes back to his own island to live. I suppose you could say, Jesus, I have really not been with anybody, except once in a while, my whole life.

Look at that nice fellow next door. Jim is a wonderful person, a respected citizen. We lived next door as good neighbors for fifteen years. Our children played together and fought together. He and I mowed each other's lawns. We would go to each other's garage and take tools to dig the garden when we needed them. I was just as close to Jim as I have ever been to anybody. Then last year his wife died. He went and lived with his oldest son ten miles away. I haven't given him a thought in six months.

We say "Hi" to the new people who moved in next door. Why haven't we had them over? "Out to lunch." It looks to me, Jesus, as if most of us were "out to lunch" to each other most of the time. The real trouble is we know we ought not to be. We *are* islands, but we're not meant to be. It ought to be that somebody needs me and he knows I'm here, that I need somebody and know he's there, and we can go to each other.

But life isn't like that. Somebody said of the patients in veterans' hospitals that seventy per cent never had anybody call on them, never received a letter or a card or a word from home. They are dead. Dead to their families, dead to everybody who knew them. They might as well be dead.

Well, here I am, pretty much unrelated to people. In my business it's not people, it's statistics, premiums. If people die, we care because we have had their money, and that's what our business is. In our personal world it's not too much better. What would happen, Jesus, do you suppose, if I were all alone in this world and there wasn't another soul on the face of the earth? Do you think the universe really would care whether I was here or not? That's a silly question. Would the universe really care if I were the last one here and were to die? Would it, Jesus? Or wouldn't it care at all?

Jesus, when you were a little boy did you ever play that game "duck on a rock"? You know, you have a gang of fellows and there are bases around the field. You get up to go on base by taking a rock and knocking a stone that's on another rock. If you do that then you get on base. But once you're on base—on the little island all alone—there's nothing you can do except wait in the hope that the next fellow who comes will knock the duck off the rock. Then you can come home free. So you wait alone, unable to do anything until the right man comes and knocks the duck off, and you're home.

Does this make sense, Jesus? Are we each of us stranded on our own little island? Can't we get any closer to each other? Can't we get home? And then you come along and knock the duck off the rock and we're home free forever? Is this maybe what you're doing up there on the cross?

You mean you aren't "out" to the thief and he isn't "out" to you? Those words you just said: "Today you will be with me in Paradise." That's a strange thing to say, Jesus. Why do you say that? Do you mean you're with him now, and you're going to be with him forever? If you're with that thief forever does that mean that you're with those veterans in hospitals forever? That you're with me forever? And with Jim and his wife who died? And the sons of my neighbors? All those people who are always "out" to everybody else? Those men and women who are going to be separated from each other from now until the day they die, are you with them too?

Are you saying something like this, Jesus—to me and everybody else—that we're "in" and not "out"? That the universe cares? That we belong? Where, Jesus, do we belong? To you?

Scene III:
On mothers and
mothers-in-law

*. . . standing by the cross of Jesus were his mother
. . . When Jesus saw his mother, and the disciple
whom he loved standing near, he said to his
mother, "Woman, behold your son!" Then he said
to the disciple, "Behold your mother!"*

JOHN 19:25-27

Jesus, that psychiatrist last summer said a strange thing. He said, "The most dangerous thing in the world is a mother's love." I had always supposed that a mother's love was the greatest thing in the world. Didn't Abraham Lincoln say that all he was he owed to his mother? Don't all good American boys honor their mothers on Mother's Day? I thought that a mother's love was the finest—not the most dangerous—thing in the world.

He went on to say that the most dangerous thing in the world was a mother's love when it was a possessive love. And I must say, as I look around me at my own family and at the families of my friends, I think that psychiatrist is right. When the mother tries to possess her children, she destroys them. Then those children, if they are ever to establish their own identity and integrity, have to stand away and say, "No! Keep your hands off." This has happened to my mother and to my children's mother and to every mother that I know about.

As a matter of fact the first argument Jane and I had was over our mothers. Whose mother were we going to on our first Christmas after we had been married—her mother or my mother? She won. The next Christmas she was pregnant so we didn't go anywhere, but we invited both sets of parents to our house. It has been that way ever since. Yet even after all these years the tug of war still goes on. Our mothers don't really like each other. Jane isn't quite good enough for my mother's son, and I'm not quite good enough for Jane's mother's daughter. How wonderful it would be if relatives could be friends instead of living in a kind of armed truce; if all six people at a wedding could be equally pleased with the marriage—the bride and groom and both sets of parents!

Why is it, Jesus, that personal relationships so often are just like this—an armed truce or a battle, somebody gets hurt, feelings are wounded, emotions become jagged and torn? Very seldom do personal relationships fit smoothly together. Jesus, why is this? As a matter of fact there's lots of real hostility. I am convinced that down deep inside my brother really hates our father. Father was always laying down the law to him, always telling him he ought to have been perfect, and he wasn't perfect. And as soon as he could, he left home. Down deep inside I'll bet he wishes father were dead.

Why are people like this, Jesus? How is it that my

sister-in-law, Jane's sister, can live with a man for twenty-five years and then suddenly up and divorce him as though they had never lived together at all, have nothing to do with him, absolutely uninterested, as though he had never lived? How can she do this with twenty-five years of her life and his together? It's a tug of war, and sometimes it's a civil war inside families.

Well, now, how did I get started on this? Oh, it was that psychiatrist—his comment about a mother's love being potentially so dangerous. "Everybody is created to love and to be loved," he said. That is the essential nature of personal relationships, especially in love and marriage. But other values get in the way. A husband wants to succeed, perhaps to impress his wife, to be able to meet her needs. So he works hard. He works so hard that he doesn't give her the time or the love or the affection he ought to.

When she doesn't get the love she expects, wants, and needs, she looks around to find someone who can give her these things. Sometimes it's another man. Usually when extramarital affairs get underway it's because something is missing in that personal relationship at home. Sometimes she goes out to work, finds—or tries to find—her satisfaction in a career. That is not bad, but the trouble with a career is that it can't love back, and something is still missing. Most often, the doctor said, the wife decides to have a baby, or if she has one, to have another. (Some wives think that as long as they keep on having babies their lives obviously have meaning. Sometimes, he said, it takes more brains not to have children than to have them.) She then turns to her children. She bestows her love on them. She smothers them with love. Afraid they will grow up too fast, she tries to keep them dependent upon her. She can't face their growing up and growing away, for then she will be all alone.

In the meantime, when the husband comes home he

wants and needs some loving too. But she is too preoccu-
pied with the children, too tired to go to bed with him, too
routinized to care. So, finally, he says the hell with it;
she's not interested in me anymore. He throws himself
back into his work, and often into the arms of his
secretary or some other woman ready to love him. So it
goes—a circle that begins slowly enough but gets faster
and tighter as the years go by. All the criss-cross loyalties
and loves, of possessing one another—or trying to. Of
loving and letting go, or of just plain losing. That's why
the psychiatrist said, "a mother's love is the most dangerous thing in the world."

Well, Jesus, these are certainly gloomy thoughts. I
never knew I had so many gloomy thoughts down deep
inside. Maybe it's because I'm in church. I've always
thought of church as a pretty gloomy place. But there are
lots of thoughts that seem to come up just while I sit here
and look at you. I see all the darkness that surrounds you
on the cross. Your story is certainly a tragedy—a good
man goes and gets killed. You are the one person who is
not, like the rest of us, separated from everybody else,
alienated, getting your feelings hurt, snapping back at
people, getting mad, sulking. You are just the opposite—
good, kind, thoughtful, loving, concerned—and here you
end up nailed to a cross.

Well, Jesus, I'd better be fair to Jane and all these other
people. I'd better be fair to all the families and the
mothers involved because obviously there is another side
to this. There is love and there is happiness and there is
joy; and we do have good times together every once in a
while. There are moments when we are genuinely concerned about each other; and there are times when life
seems to come together and all the empty broken pieces
are picked up and put together again. Many times I don't
know what I would have done without Jane's mother
helping us. I don't know what I would have done without

her and her care when I had that little heart attack two years ago. I've seen her care a thousand times.

So there really is another side to what that psychiatrist said about possessive love being the worst thing in the world. The other side must be that the best thing in the world is love that doesn't try to possess, love that doesn't try to hold on to somebody else. Maybe that's the most creative thing in the world. What about that, Jesus? Is that why you're up there, because you refuse to possess anybody?

Who has helped me most in my life? Not those people who tried to possess me or straighten me out or own me or control me, but those who have been concerned primarily with helping me to establish myself, to be myself and stand on my own ground, to be a free person, not owned, even with the best intentions, by anybody else.

Isn't that true in all these family relationships? A mother or father who tries to possess a child finds that the child will try to break away and stand on his own feet, and that the relationship will be broken and hostility will take over. But the more the parents try not to possess their children, and try to help them stand on their own two feet, the sooner those children grow and return that love as mature adults.

I remember a picnic we went on when our youngest child was five years old. After lunch she climbed up on a little cliff and shouted to us that she couldn't get down. I said, "If you got up there, you can get down." Jane wanted me to go get her and carry her down. So we argued. Finally, we went and stood at the foot of the cliff and encouraged her, told her where to put her feet. She came down by herself. It was more painful for us not helping her than if we had helped her, but it was the only way we could help her learn to trust herself and to stand on her own two feet.

If we really love someone, we don't try to own them. We can't own anybody. And the more we love them the more we want to set them free from us—to help them stand on their own ground in their own selves. We can stand under them, loving them, but we can't live for them. That's real pain, Jesus, when you love like that.

You must be suffering pain up there, Jesus. Maybe it's only through the pain of this experience that you can really show your love for us. Maybe this is the only way you can set us free and put us on our own ground so we can grow and mature and love you freely. You never overpower us with your love, do you, Jesus? You don't come into our lives to possess us unless we want to be possessed, do you? Your love is something like the love of a parent for a child—to set us free so we can be supported by that love and grow with it and love in return. That cross, that love, must be pain. Maybe love can only express itself through pain—to set free the people we love.

Those words you just said, Jesus: "Woman, behold your Son . . . [Son] behold your mother." Well, Jesus, here's my mother and Jane's mother and my father and Jane's father, our children, my brother, his wife, my sister, her divorced husband, their children, all their family, all the families in all the nice neighborhoods, all those in the not-so-nice neighborhoods, all the families in all the world, all fathers, mothers, brothers, sisters, mothers-in-law, fathers-in-law, uncles, aunts, children— all members of each other.

Your love is painful, I guess, but all love is painful, isn't it, Jesus? Isn't this the only way your love can ever finally set us free to love each other? Is this what you are trying to say on the cross? "Who is my mother, who are my brothers? Behold my mother and my brothers!"

Does this describe you, Jesus? "Love is patient and kind. Love is not jealous or boastful; it is not arrogant or rude. Love does not insist on its own way; it is not irritable or resentful; it does not rejoice at wrong, but rejoices in the right. Love bears all things, believes all things, hopes all things, endures all things."

Is that what you're doing up there on the cross?

Is that what you *are*?

Scene IV:
Dialogue of despair

"My God, my God, why hast thou forsaken me?"

MARK 15:34

It's interesting, Jesus, what a man thinks about when he sits down quietly and just looks at you, what half-forgotten thoughts come back to him—what ideas, what fears, what hidden hopes now become gradually exposed.

To be perfectly honest though, I don't often stir these muddy waters. It's too frightening to see what's hidden down in those depths. Maybe that's why I went to see the psychiatrist when I was so depressed last summer. I couldn't face it alone.

Maybe that's why I don't seem to mind so much sitting here under the cross in your presence. I need company

85

when I look inside. And you've been through this before.
You looked down into the bottom of my heart long ago,
didn't you, Jesus? I'm not telling you anything you don't
already know. How many people have unburdened their
hearts to you, Jesus, and to nobody else? How many
hearts have you looked down into from the top of that
cross? A million? A billion? A trillion? An infinite number?
Because each person knows in his own inner loneliness
that you had the same thing, you, above all other people,
were somehow with them when they were afraid, with
them as nobody else could ever be.

When things really went wrong, and they obviously
went wrong for you a lot of times, did you ever think of
suicide, Jesus? Was it suicide when you let yourself go to
that cross? Why did you let that happen? When things
went wrong in your life, you certainly must have thought
of giving up and saying, "What's the use? Those people
will never understand what I'm here for." Did you finally
come to the end of your rope?

What causes people to commit suicide, Jesus? That's a
stupid question. I suppose there are as many reasons as
there are people who do it, or think about doing it. And
who can tell, anyway? Who can tell about what goes
on—*really* goes on—in somebody else's mind? We can
hardly tell what goes on in our own.

I think there must be devastating loneliness. There
must be that deep awful sense that there is really no use
going on, no purpose left in life, if there ever was one. And
it's hard to tell why that should be. Some people who
commit suicide are not loved, others are. Some are
successful, others are failures. Some come from broken
homes, others from secure homes. Sometimes suicide
seems simply like giving up in despair, and at other times
like looking back in anger. Some do it because self-pity
overcomes them, others because love does. God knows. I
sure don't know.

I almost committed suicide once. Last winter—Tuesday night, the night after that storm. Remember that storm all weekend long? I came into the office on Tuesday morning when I didn't have to. My boss asked me to come in; he said he had some news for me. Why he took that day to break the news when we all should have been patted on the back for coming to the office, I'll never know. It was no day to knock a man down, but that was the day I almost committed suicide. My boss was going to retire in June. For ten years he'd been grooming me to take his place. When he would step down, then I would step up. I knew his job better than he did. That morning he said, "John, I have bad news for you. Our division is going to merge with the Chicago division and the man in Chicago is going to come here and take over after Easter."

Well, he really didn't have to go on. He tried to say, "Look, it's really better this way. You know the job. You won't have any new responsibilities to worry about. You can have all your regular accounts. You can enjoy life." But I knew what had happened. I wasn't going to the top, after all. I'd been passed over. I was right where I was going to stay for the next eighteen years. Eighteen years of nothing to do. I was finished.

Well, I was pretty good at dinner that night. I kept up appearances, told a few jokes, and after dinner I told Jane that I was going to go and help a couple of fellows who had been stuck in the snow down near Fairview Lane. So I went out of the house and turned the other way toward the Golf Club—and I walked. It was a beautiful night, almost no traffic. Once in a while a car would go by with its chains clanking: snow was all over the place, everything subdued. It was like a fairyland. It was cold. There was a bright half-moon, and the clouds moved slowly across it. When it came through, it lit up all the sides of the hill where the twelfth and thirteenth fairways are. I

sat on the fence along the twelfth fairway and I looked
out over the snow—cold, bleak, beautiful. There was no
sound except occasional shouts from the other side of the
club house where some children were sliding down the
hill. I sat alone and I thought.

There wasn't any use getting mad. There was nobody
to get mad at. My boss had done what he could. I was
sure that the man in Chicago had hardly ever heard of me.
Just one of those big, impersonal shuffles that takes place.
Well, I thought, I'll resign and get out and I'll start all over
again somewhere else. They can't trap me here for the
next eighteen years. Then I thought: I can't do that, not
with all the deductions and the insurance and the pension
payments. I would lose everything if I just turned around
and walked out now.

Then I thought, well, I'd be better off—the whole family
would be better off—if I were dead. If I just gave up now
—and I'm really finished anyway—Jane would get all
that money. She'd be sorry, and the children would be
sorry. The neighbors would be sorry, too. They'd say it
was temporary insanity. "Too bad," they'd say. "John
was such a good fellow. What a terrible thing! He must
have been depressed. Why couldn't we see what was
going on?" Then in a few months, at most a few years,
they'd get over it. They'd remember just the best things
about me, the jokes, the good times we had.

There wasn't anybody to go to that night. Nobody at
home, nobody at the office. It never occurred to me to go
to a church. I don't know how long I sat there. It was as
though I had gradually become numb and frozen. The
moon was hidden behind the clouds and the wind came
up. I began to cry. I hadn't cried like that since I was
seven years old. That place looked like the end of the
world, nothing but frozen, bleak landscape forever, for
the next eighteen years. I thought, "Why don't you shoot

yourself? The gun is in the garage. You know where the shells are." But I didn't. Why didn't I?

You said, "My God, my God, why hast thou forsaken me?" That's just how I felt. But I didn't say anything to God that night. I never thought of him. If I'd said "My God," at least I'd have been talking to *somebody*. But on that fence that night there was nothing but cold, wet, frozen nothingness. And I was engulfed in it.

But if you can say, "My God," then at least there is somebody you can talk to, somebody, even if he's forsaken you and is beating you up. Somebody is better than nobody. That whole frozen wasteland of nothing, that was terrible. "My God, my God."

You know, Jesus, maybe there's somebody who does share this despair. Maybe just you and me. Maybe you, me, and everybody else who's ever had this same frozen nothingness.

"My God." Maybe that's why I didn't commit suicide last winter. Maybe so I could sit here this afternoon and find you in exactly the same fix I was in. Does that sound fantastic? At the end of the road, a failure, finished, defeated, forsaken, nobody left to care whether you live or die. And so you cry to God.

If he's your God, Jesus, then maybe he's mine. You know, this may be as low as a man can ever get, depressed to nothingness. I hope I can say, "My God." If I can say, "My God," then I must be here right now for some reason. "My God, my God!" Is it true Jesus that you are where you are up there on that cross because that is where God wants you to be? Do you think it's true that I'm where I am because this is where he wants me to be? "My God, my God."

Scene V:
Aching, longing, yearning

"I thirst"

JOHN 19:28

Well, Jesus, I think now I've told you almost everything that has swelled up from the bottom of my heart. I've told you about my family and my friends. I've told you about my sins and frustrations and failures. I've even boasted about some of my accomplishments. After all, I have done a pretty reasonable job with my life. But I haven't told you about the aching I carry around in my heart all the time. It's an aching or a longing or a yearning with me all the time, and it's probably closer to my real inner self than anything else.

I don't know if I can tell you about it, because I'm not sure what it is myself. I wouldn't mind telling you, if I could. That in itself is something. I never, I suppose, really thought about telling you anything before this afternoon. I just never thought much about you. What I remembered about you from Sunday School I didn't like very much. "Jesus, tender shepherd, hear me. Bless thy little lamb tonight." That was soupy, icky. I didn't want to be a lamb. I wanted to be a wolf—a six-year-old wolf. Later I thought of you always judging me. You were a policeman with a big stick and you went around saying, "Don't do this! Don't do that!" And those were always the things I wanted to do. So I was pretty happy when I finally outgrew you, and I said to myself, "The hell with it! Life is what you make it. Stand up and be a man and stop simpering around!" Why I ever associated simpering with you, I don't know. You certainly aren't simpering now.

I hope I'm not simpering. I'm trying to get at this ache. There is that thing inside me trying to get out. Sometimes, I think I'm going to burst, I am so filled with it. It's painful. Yet it's not just a great big pain sitting there doing nothing. It's there for some reason.

It's yearning for something. It's wanting something. It's wanting to be related to something, to touch something beyond myself. It's searching for something to be caught up in. Once in a while I'll identify with a painting. "There," I'll say. "That's it. That really turns me on." Somehow I get into that painting. Or I see a picture of a wave crashing on the beach and I come in on that wave. It breaks over me and I belong to it. Sometimes this sense of being carried along comes with music. I'm at the symphony, not thinking of much. Then Bach's music—or Beethoven's, more likely—crashes in, carries me away. I belong somewhere else. I *am*. While the music lasts I am, as they say, transported. When it stops, I let myself drift. I am sorry when the trance ends and I have to stand up and go out. Even applause seems somehow out of place.

I never can tell when this mood is going to hit me, or

what triggers it. It seems to bring sadness and joy together. It's as though I were being reminded that I really belonged somewhere else, and something was trying to carry me there.

Some evenings when the sun goes down and the colors spread over the sky, they seem to touch me, lift me, color me, possess me. I had the same experience on a ship during the war. I was standing up in the bow of that transport way the hell and gone out in the Pacific. The ship rose, fell, rolled, and the waves came rushing over the bow. I took the spray in my face. Refreshed, I seemed to become part of the ship, part of the water—part of creation almost. At times like that the pain is so great you think you are going crazy. But you know you're not because you are somehow most satisfied at the same time. You are fulfilled. I guess that's what it is. You are *you!* Bang! Right there in the middle of existence, and even if there is terror, it's more like awe and you're ok.

You get it with people sometimes. You meet somebody —a man or a woman—and it's as though you knew each other immediately. You are both perfectly there, all there. You belong to each other. You just know there is something more in that relationship than meets the eye. You sense that you belong to each other, know each other, have known each other maybe forever, even love each other. But more than that, you sense you belong to something more than each other. You know you are known—and not just by that other person. Somehow you are safe and loved, and that's what the hell life is all about. It's yearning, aching for that; that's what I'm talking about, Jesus. God, how can I ever find this? How can I ever get it?

This yearning is desire and pain and joy all in one. It's a longing, Jesus, that nobody seems able to satisfy—at least not for long. Can you really satisfy it?

You cry now, "I thirst." That's strange. What do you

thirst for? What do I thirst for? I wonder if somehow down deep inside I haven't been thirsty for you—or for God—or someone. Is it you I have been running away from all these years? My God, I have been running! That's for sure! But at least right now, I'm turning toward you. Are you the one I've been reaching for?

I remember that prayer: "Our hearts are restless until they rest in thee." How come I remember that, Jesus? I don't even know when I learned it. It came to me gradually last summer when the psychiatrist had done all he could (and, God knows, he did all he could!) that there was something else, something more trying to get at me through him. The more I thought about it, the more I wondered if there wasn't a spirit that was somehow tied up with you and with everybody who was trying to do any healing in the world. It wasn't just the psychiatrist, wise as he was, it was more than that—maybe his commitment to his discipline—that made it possible for healing to go on. Once I even said "O.K. God. You do it."

Do you think that was God last summer, Jesus? Was that you? Or am I crazy? Is there some Thing, some One at work in all the people and forces who bring life and healing and strength? Is there a Power saying yes to us to make us whole? Is that you, Jesus? Is that what I am yearning for? You?

There is another thing that's even harder to talk about. It is the search for beauty outside myself and a wondering about beauty inside myself. What is the relation between that beauty, which I long to be a part of in other things and other people, and the state of my soul inside. It has to do with the longing and the love and the pain and the joy I have with other people. How do you keep the beauty of that spirit which holds us, keep within it, express it, and live wholly at the same time? Is it true, Jesus, that such beauty is, finally, in holiness, and that if there is no holiness there is no beauty? So when I talk about the vision of beauty for myself, that I hold for myself, there won't be any unless I become holy? Is this true?

Who is going to do that? How do you become holy? How do I begin? Is this yearning and desire that brought me here a beginning?

Do you suppose I could ever say that I long for you, Jesus. Whoever would have known that I might even think that my longing was for you? What do you say? What do you say, Jesus? Is it *you* I long for?

Scene VI:
So it goes

"It is finished"

JOHN 19:30

"It is finished." That sounds like the refrain in *Slaughterhouse Five*. Kurt Vonnegut describes the horrors we've experienced in my generation, and after each one he says, "So it Goes." In the fire-bombing of Dresden, 35,000 people were killed. "So it goes." He writes about the Second World War and about Vietnam and about death, and he always ends, "So it goes." The last chapter begins like this:

Robert Kennedy . . . was shot two nights ago. He died last night. So it goes.

Martin Luther King was shot a month ago. He died too. So it goes.

And every day my Government gives me an account of corpses created by military science in Vietnam. So it goes.

My father died many years ago of natural causes. So it goes.

He was a sweet man. He was a gun nut, too. He left me his guns
—they rust.[1]

Fatalism—it's pretty hard not to think you're trapped.
Some people live wonderful, outgoing, loving lives—and
death comes. Other men are out for all they can get.
Death doesn't come. The good suffer, and the evil get off
scott free. And I'm not the greatest. There are a lot worse
off than I.

I remember when my college roommate's wife called
up one summer vacation and I said, "Hi, how's Jim?" And
she said, "He's dead!" What kind of sense does that make,
Jesus?

Maybe you're the only one I put that question to. What
sense does that death make? Why all this suffering? What
did you do when those people murmured against you?
Peter said he would never let you down. Then the minute
your back was turned, he denied you three times. Everybody you trusted failed you. And now such terrible
physical pain. Soon you'll be dead, finished, your suffering finished. "So it goes."

Well, I can't sit here looking at you on the cross,
knowing you'll soon be dead and just shrug it off. I can't
just say, "Yes, that's the way life is. Too bad. When your
number is up, it's up. Nothing you can do about it. So it
goes."

How can I get inside what you're doing up there? How
can I make any sense of what it means? How come you of
all people—the best—have to go through the dying
process? Obviously what you're doing made a difference
in the world. I wouldn't be here if it hadn't. None of the
others would be here either. How come there is that
power that seems to come out from the cross and from
you and attracts people? You give us something that
doesn't seem to come through other people's deaths.

You are finishing now what you came to do, whatever

that was. I guess it was to be God in the world. That's as blunt as I can put it. That is, to be love in the world. God was in you, and you were love. So what happens? You get crucified. Love dies. You die.

You die up there because you had to be true to your nature. You *had* to be yourself; that is what God wanted you to be. When you obey love as the only way you can be yourself, you also have to take all the things that are against love, like hate and fear and selfishness and sin and all the rest. That's just the way life is. That's how it is. So it goes. You die. Of course.

How come this difference, then? We're not sitting here just to see again that love gets it in the neck, or that all men die, and your death is just sadder because you were such a good man. No, there has to be more to it than that.

The only way I can figure it is that you willingly, almost eagerly, let yourself die because this was the *only* way you could love God. And if it is God you are loving and God is love, then it isn't all over with God or you. There is more. You come back. Or love comes back. Or God comes back. This death isn't the end. If it were, we'd never be here now. You have come back and you've said, "Look, if you want to get in on the secret, come, take a look at my death on the cross, and then get on with your own life, your own decisions. You take your own crosses. Do that and you will find that you keep on going with more strength. Try just taking whatever your pain is because you have to be true to your nature. Be true to love, and see if you don't come back too. You're supposed to be risen yourself. You will be if you live with the spirit here in me on the cross: obeying love, trusting God."

So you can say, "It is finished" because that is the end of your human life. But maybe I can say "It is beginning" because I'm just beginning to try to live in accordance with your will for me.

Is that how it goes?

Scene VII:
Point of no return

"Father, into thy hands I commit my spirit."

LUKE 23:46

Well, Jesus, it's almost three o'clock. Soon I'll be going home. Where are you going? Well, I suppose, in a sense you're going home too. I suppose you're going home, home to your Father where you came from in the first place. Maybe one of the reasons you came to live with us was to remind us that we have another home. We don't really belong here forever. We are temporary inhabitants, who live out our lives as well as we can and then when we finish we go back home. That home is life with you and your father. Does that make any sense? Anyway, if you are committing your spirit into the hands of your Father he must be ready to take it—and eventually to take us too.

You know, Jesus, once when I was nineteen I stepped on a nail and got blood poisoning and almost died. I was out on an island. By the time I finally got to the hospital I was out of it. I came to with a raging fever. As I looked around at the walls and gradually collected myself, it was as though I were climbing up a long steep stairway from a well that went all the way down into nothing. I had been down there. I was just beginning to climb back up. That was the point of my death. Then I thought to myself, "Well, now at least, I know what it's like to die." You go to a certain point right down to the bottom and there's no return. The point of no return is to die. And you know what it felt like? Nothing. Just the end.

Well, I was just finishing the climb out of the well and I knew I was not dead, but I knew what dying was like. As I came to, I turned my head and there was a man in the next bed. He looked like an old man. He said, "Hi." I said, "Hi." Then he said, "Would you do me a favor?" I said, "Sure." He said, "Ring that bell for the nurse, will you?" So I said, "Sure." I rang for the nurse and she came in. He said, "I am going to die now. Would you read the Twenty-third Psalm to me?" She said, "No, I'll get the doctor." She turned to me and she said, "Here, you read it." So I read it.

"The Lord is my shepherd; I shall not want. He maketh me to lie down in green pastures. He leadeth me beside the still waters . . ." As I began to read the doctors came in. The man said, "Keep reading."

So I went on. "He restoreth my soul; he leadeth me in the paths of righteousness for his name's sake. Yea, though I walk through the valley of the shadow of death, I will fear no evil, for thou art with me; thy rod and thy staff they comfort me. Thou preparest a table before me in the presence of mine enemies; thou anointest my head with oil; my cup runneth over—surely goodness and mercy shall follow me all the days of my life and I shall dwell in the house of the Lord forever." When I had finished, he was dead.

I thought: why all this fuss? There's nothing to it. You just die. But I was wrong, wasn't I, Jesus? You don't just die. You go home. Isn't that why you said, "Father, into thy hands I commit my spirit"?

Some meeting place, Jesus, for a fellow like me! Here I've poured out my heart and I've given you my hopes. And in a way, I feel you've poured out your heart to me. At least you've given me a glimpse of the mystery of why you're on the cross. You have drawn me into another world of knowing and being known, of being both afraid and safe, where suffering is bearable, where the world is joyous and it's just fun to be. That's your world as it is; that's your world.

Now you're going home. So am I—to the home where there is some fun in living, right along with all the sorrow and sadness; a home where there is a mainstream of love that carries me along even though I don't ever do it very well. You're going home and I'm going home. Is there anything better than this, Jesus?

You know, I am feeling a little of the excitement I felt when I came home from camp when I was twelve—the excitement of going home. I knew that my mother and my father would be glad that I was there. Even my brothers. My mother would have pork chops with apples and asparagus, and vanilla ice cream with strawberries for dessert. But best of all was *being* there. Everybody glad I was there; and I was glad they were.

You're going home to your father, who will be glad to see you. I'm going home and will be glad to see my family. They'll be glad to see me and maybe some day we'll make a world where everybody will be glad that everybody is.

But the best thing about going home is, I'll meet you

there. I'll be with you and you'll be glad to see me. I'll be glad to see you.

Jesus, "into your hands I commit my spirit."

May we be at home in you—all of us—forever.

Epilogue:
Drawn into God

The phrase "drawn into God" is simply a way of describing what cannot be described—one's "hidden" life in God. "Let me hide myself in Thee" is the way an old hymn puts it. "Our life is hid with Christ in God" is the way St. Paul puts it. Or, "we are buried with Christ in his death" on Good Friday that we may be made "partakers of his resurrection" on Easter Day. Nobody can see this inner drawing into God, nor can it ever be described. It is hidden. It can be summarized only within oneself, hiddenly with God.

How do you summarize this hidden life of your own with God? Your interior life? How does your dialogue with God go? Does he, through your conversations with him, draw you into himself? Do you become a part of him, participate *in* him? Do you—in a curious, mysterious way—become God? Is that fantasy? Or heresy? Or the deepest truth of all? In his own interior dialogue with his Father,

Jesus said, "I pray . . . for those who believe in me, that as thou, Father, art in me and I in thee, that they also may be in us, so that the world may believe that thou hast sent me." That prayer is being answered as we are being drawn into him.

You hear a bird sing. It is twilight, or dawn is breaking. You are outside. The bird sings a song. You say to yourself, "That is a beautiful song. He is singing that song for me. He lifts my spirit; my heart is warmed; I am welcomed by him. He is calling me, doing something to me."

Then you think, "That's silly. The bird is just singing. He is singing because that is his nature. That is just what birds do. To be a bird is to sing. Why then is my spirit lifted and my heart warmed; and why do I feel welcomed? What is there in me that is responding this way to that song? Is this God lifting my heart, warming me, drawing me?"

I don't know. I can say, "No, that's not God. That is just a bird." But what is there within me that is warmed by the song, drawn and called, that makes more of me and that was there before he sang to me? I can say, "No, that is not God." But I can also say, "Yes, that is God. That is the spirit of God." Then I can say, "*You,* God, are you calling me, drawing me. God, tell me." The reply comes, "Why do you think you are speaking to me, except I have come to draw you to myself? The song is the song of the universe. Creation sings. That note is me. You belong to that. So sing."

Or, you ask, "Where is God?" The answer is, "God is everywhere." You ask God, "Are you here?" He answers, "Where else can I be?" You say, "Thank you." Then after a time, you say "I'm going now," and as you say it you hear him say, "Me too."

Have you ever been shattered by life—just shattered? Death, failure, brokenness, injustice, everything tumbles around you and life is crashed and you crash? You have nothing, are nothing; you have been broken in pieces and you cry, "God, why?" And the answer comes: "Why not? Who do you think you are that you should be exempt from the pain and the agony of creation? How else can I draw you but by the shattering of your pride of yourself— of you? Who do you think you are—God? No, I am God. You are you—the one I love, and I am shattered with you. So come, together we'll rise from the dead." And you do.

To move into God is to begin, however feebly, to look at creation—the beauty of it, the fallen nature it has (human nature, our broken selfish nature as well as the natural evil that rampages on its own destructive way). To move into God is to begin to look upon this creation from inside rather than from outside. It is to sense that we belong within nature, that we share its pain in order that we can share its glory at the same time, that we are possessed by it, that we belong to it. It owns us; we do not own it.

To be drawn into God is to belong to all that happens. A bird's song is God drawing us to see we belong to him. A flash of insight that God is with us at that moment, the sense of it, the power of it—drawing us to see that the flashes are eternal and that they shoot through every moment of time. To be caught up in time is to be caught up in eternity—God.

To be shattered is to be crucified. The world is shattered. Humanity is shattered. I am shattered. We belong to that ongoing humanity that is broken. God so loved this world—humankind—that he is shattered with it. That cross, above all else, shows how shattered he is. It is the shattering that draws men to him. As we accept and share the shattering for which we are in part responsible, then we share the glory as well as the agony.

It is a curious mixture. We seem to be made for both joy and pain. They often—perhaps always—are joined together. You love somebody, for example, and are transported with joy; at the same time you ache because you cannot love adequately. Or, you lose someone you love, and suffer great pain. You ache for that person, but in that aching you may come to know a deeper joy than before. Death, and all the pain that surrounds the loss of people we love, seems often to be the only way we can be carried into another dimension of life which gives us a broader, higher perspective upon our existence. When the joy and the pain are woven together, we find the fabric of life has richer hues.

The cross sets this ambiguous mixture clearly before us: life and death, pain and joy belong together. We don't get joy without love, and pain, with love, can move into joy. The cross makes it clear that living and loving belong together, and so do agony and glory. At the heart of life there is both love and pain. The circle of the universe of existence is held together by two beams—one vertical and one horizontal, making the cross. The cross is centered in the circle. From that cross, Christ is drawing us to himself. Focus on him there and he draws us through on to the other side where there is perfect—whole—love, joy, and glory. That is breaking through all the pain and clouds into the radiance of Easter Day.

So, longing for life is longing for God. And we long for him because he longs for us. He draws us to him through all the experiences of life—the broken and the whole. He is taking you into himself to bring you to a yet more glorious day when you shall be partaker of his resurrection, bursting forth in that glory to be in God—one with God—forever and ever.

> *Christ,*
> *You who draw all men*
> *now into yourself,*
> *draw us.*
> *You who on the Cross*

gave yourself
because you loved
your father and us,
draw us.
You who consumed into yourself
all hates, separations, sin
and death,
and turned them into nothing
with no power left,
draw us.
You who on the Cross
drew from the darkness
the eternal light
that lightens every man,
draw us
into that glorious light
that bursts from
your incredible grace and love
now and always

Amen.

PART III

In Resurrection

11

The Godspell *message*[1]

*G*odspell is the long-running off-Broadway play, a bouncy movie and popular recording that attempts to communicate the Gospel in a youthful idiom for the seventies. It seeks to cut through much of the mustiness, stuffiness, and formality that make it difficult for the Gospel to be heard in formal church services.

Here, for example, is *Godspell*'s translation of one of the stories told by Jesus:

> There once was a rich man
> whose land yielded heavy crops.
> He debated with himself:
> "Oh what am I to do?" he said,
> "I will tear down my storehouses
> and build them bigger.
> I will collect in them all my corn,
> and popcorn,
> and tuna surprise,
> and M & M's,
> and then I will say to myself,
> "Man, you have plenty of good things laid by you,

109

enough to last you many years. Take life easy.
Eat. Drink. Enjoy yourself."
But then God said to the man,
"You fool, this very night
you must surrender your life.
You have made your money.
Who will get it now?"

It is, however, not simply a matter of translating Bible verses into contemporary language that brings this freshness, although that helps. Much of the play's language is, in fact, quite traditional. Psalm 103, for example, is translated:

O bless the Lord, my soul
His grace to thee proclaim
And all that is within me join
To bless his holy name.

There is also the musical setting—soft rock—which catches the mood of the seventies. It is simple, very simple, with a strong beat, easy to follow, very easy to be caught up by, to be possessed by, and to express oneself in.

There is a litany, "We beseech thee, hear us." Listen to this litany's lyrics:

Father, hear Thy children's call
Humbly at Thy feet we fall
Prodigals, confessing all
We beseech Thee, hear us

Come sing about love, that caused us first to be
Come sing about love, that made the stone and tree
Come sing about love, love, love that draws us lovingly
We beseech Thee, hear us

The song, "Day by Day," is one of the most tender, moving expressions of Christian devotion ever composed:

Day by Day—
Oh, dear Lord, three things I pray
To see thee more clearly
Love thee more dearly
Follow thee more nearly
Day by day

The words are from thirteenth-century England and were put into the 1940 hymnal (Hymn 429) with two tunes prepared particularly for that hymnal. Most people who sing "Day by Day" think it was an original composition written for *Godspell*, so well do the words and the music fit together.

So there are words, there is music, and there is a message. Put most simply, the message is "God and people." Not God and churches; not God and states; not God and a good, safe, gray, murky Jesus; not God embalmed in a tomb of orthodoxy or preserved in a frozen, formal liturgy; but a living God concerned with living people.

When wilt thou save the people?
O God of mercy, when?
The people, Lord, the people
Not thrones and crowns, but men!
God save the people, for Thine they are,
Thy children, as Thy angels fair
Save the people from despair
God save the people
God save the people
God save the people

The people are saved by the Savior. In *Godspell*, when the Savior, Jesus Christ, comes, he comes as a clown. He makes fun of the externals—the pomp, the outside of the cup, the legalisms, the Pharisees, the conformists—in order to make crystal clear the inner core of the Gospel. He makes fun of the jumbled irrationalities of life. He takes the disjointedness of human existence and laughs so that we may not take either our virtues or our failures too seriously. He helps us laugh at life and at ourselves.

The laughter comes very close to joy. It is a happy play. In the laughter and the songs, there is a confident assurance that despite all the mess that the world and our own lives are in, God is in the world and in us. He loves it; he loves us; and he will save his people.

The joyful, funny, loving, compassionate, outgoing, listening young players communicate very naturally with the audience. By the end of the evening, there are no players and no audience, but simply one company of people praising the Lord, praising life, loving one another, accepting one another, forgiving one another, and living —if only for that magic moment: the Gospel According to St. Matthew. Life is good. Its goodness rests upon the people who are secure enough in their faith to love, accept, forgive, and belong to one another. We are all humans who share the experience of walking this earth together—that is the message of *Godspell*. The medium by which that message is communicated becomes, in fact, the message itself.

The message is a judgment on the Church because in comparison with *Godspell*, most productions put forth by the Church are just plain dreary. They are too often solemn, frozen, and formal, with no joy or lift and with little enthusiasm or movement.

But *Godspell* also brings hope. It makes clear the deep, hidden, religious instinct of people today. That instinct is hidden, perhaps, under great layers of agnosticism, cynicism, and materialism, but down deep it is still there. There is a yearning and a longing for life to have some meaning, a yearning and a longing to be able to relate to one's fellow travelers, a yearning and a longing to be able to affirm life joyfully. It is there—a joy that bubbles up when it is given an opportunity.

It is a spirit of people touching one another, reaching

out for one another, accepting and having concern for one another, and being happy about life as they go about living it.

The subtitle of *Godspell* is "A musical adaptation of the Gospel According to St. Matthew." How true is it to St. Matthew?

There are twenty-eight chapters in Matthew's Gospel. The final chapter is the climax of the story of Jesus. It tells what happened after the crucifixion: how Jesus was raised from the dead; how he appeared again to his disciples; how he commissioned them to go teach what they have learned from him. Matthew ends with the words of Jesus, "I shall be with you always."

Godspell ends with the crucifixion. The finale sets Jesus on the cross, and his last words are, "O God, I'm dead." He is then taken down from the cross. His disciples lift him, put him on their shoulders and cry out, "Long live God!" Then they carry the corpse up the steps and out of the theatre singing the song with which the play begins, "Prepare Ye the Way of the Lord"—the song of John the Baptist, who prepares the people for the coming Jesus.

That is the way *Godspell* ends. St. Matthew's Gospel ends this way:

Early on Sunday morning before dawn, Mary Magdalene and the other Mary ran down to the sepulchre to begin to prepare the body of Jesus for anointing. As they approached they felt the tremors of an earthquake. When they came to the tomb they found that the stone that had blocked the entrance of the tomb had been rolled away and an angel was sitting on it. The angel said, Don't be afraid. Jesus is risen as he said he was going to be. Go back and tell the disciples that he has been raised from the dead and that he will meet them in Galilee.

So they hurried back. On the way they were suddenly confronted with Jesus who said, "Do not be afraid. Go and tell my brothers they must leave for Galilee, and there they will see me."

In the final scene in the Gospel we see eleven disciples gathered on a mountain top as Jesus appears before them. Then this interesting sentence: "When they saw him, they worshipped him, *but some doubted.*"

He gives them what is called the Great Commission: "Go, baptize and teach the truth to all the nations that they may learn the commandments that I have taught you to obey." And his final words were, "I will be with you always." That is his promise—the end of the chapter, the end of the Gospel.

The climax of the Gospel is Jesus raised from the dead, his appearance to his disciples, and his giving them that commission. The Gospel is the Gospel of the resurrection. The good news of the Gospel is that Jesus has been raised from the dead and has overcome death. That is the Church's message to the world. To make that proclamation clear to the world is the reason the Church was founded. It is a message to be proclaimed by people who have that faith, who believe it, and who live it.

In Christian celebration, we do not simply gather together to have a good time; we are celebrating something specific. We are celebrating the resurrection and the joyful warm, human fellowship derived from it.

How can we do justice to that message today? How can that Gospel best be conveyed in the theatre? If you were the author of *Godspell* and wanted to write a finale that corresponded with Matthew's finale, how would you present it? You might try to give a literal representation of the resurrection appearances and of the meeting of Jesus with his disciples. You could use all the magic arts that the theatre possesses to do that: lights, music, costumes, sets. You could create the illusion of an angel sitting on a rock, then Jesus meeting the women and, finally, appearing on the mountain top and commissioning his disciples. The audience, having seen this representation of the resurrection of Jesus, would leave the theatre saying, "We saw him with our own eyes—the resurrected Jesus. So we believe he is raised from the dead. He was right there in that role played by that nice young actor."

This kind of literal interpretation seems to me to debase the element of faith, the element that is required to see the risen Christ. The Christian lives by faith and he doesn't need or expect or even want a literal Christ rising physically from the dead. But there is another and I think a better way, to communicate the resurrection faith.

It would be to try to capture on stage the faith of the disciples. You would not need to have Christ appear. In fact you would not want it. (If it could be demonstrated that Christ was risen from the dead, then you would not need faith to see him.) The scene would be set on the mountain top. The disciples are gathered together, drawn by the spirit of Jesus, responding to that spirit as they remember what he was like when he walked the earth. They are convinced that the love they now have for one another cannot be contained but has to be spread throughout the whole world. Bursting with the conviction that Christ is still with them in spirit, they set out to proclaim that love to the nations of the world, "He is risen. Obey him. Follow his teachings. Love one another and you will rise to new life. That is our faith—our faith in Christ risen."

Then the curtain would fall upon the disciples worshipping him, except for "some" who "doubted."

This way of staging the resurrection underlines the crucial difference that is made by a "community of believers." A community of believers bound together in a fellowship of the spirit makes it possible for individuals to have the spirit dwell within them.

These are two alternatives (you might think of others) —one literal, one of faith. The author of *Godspell* did it differently. We leave the theatre having been exposed to the teachings of Jesus, his parables and the stories he told. We see him die. We hear the shout, "Long live God." The body is carried out of the theatre. Jesus is dead.

Godspell ends with the song, "Prepare Ye the Way of the Lord." *You* prepare the way. The risen Lord appears when we prepare the way for him to appear.

Do you have faith in the risen Jesus? If you don't, do you want it? If you want the faith, the way to get it is to prepare his way by living his life. *Godspell* describes that life: love of God, love of neighbor, love of oneself. It is in living him that you come to see him. It is in living him that you *become* him. He is risen to a new life because you are. It rests upon your preparation. That is the good news— infinite hope for us for a new life because *he* is raised from the dead.

The Lord comes because you prepare his way. How he comes is for you to decide. If you decide he doesn't come, he doesn't. He comes when you decide. He comes when you forgive someone, when you do your utmost to be reconciled to someone, when you express your deep sorrow that you have hurt someone. He comes when you accept with compassion, when you are willing to sacrifice something of yourself—your time, your money—for someone who needs it. That is preparing the way. It is out of your life, your acts, that he comes and rises again—and again and again.

So the Finale of *Godspell* is written in your life and your living.

So go now; live the Gospel; write your own conclusion to it; live your own Gospel. It will become the Gospel of the Lord Jesus who, he promises, will be with you always, even to the end of the world.

12

Resurrection NOW

How shall we, in the late twentieth century, make sense out of Christ's resurrection from the dead? Is it possible, with any kind of integrity, to make our own that Easter greeting of the primitive Church: "He is risen. He is risen, indeed."? How is the modern mind to deal honestly with the mystery of new life rising out of old deaths?

There is only one way. It is to live a resurrected life yourself. It is to be risen, to let yourself be risen. It is not to try to raise yourself. No man can do that. Christ could not do that. But you can set the conditions that make it possible for your life to be raised.

There was a man once whose daughter had a mental breakdown at twenty-one and was institutionalized for the rest of her life. When he was asked what it meant, he said: "I do not know. But never again will I ever say an unkind word about anybody." And he never did. Kindness arising out of tragedy. Life out of death.

There was another man whose wife died in an automobile accident. When he was asked what it meant, he replied: "I do not know. But my heart goes out to everyone who has a burden and I have simply got to be a more responsible citizen than I ever was." Integrity arising out of bereavement. New life out of death.

A marriage is dying. Alienation is growing, getting worse and worse. Adultery takes place. The one who does not commit adultery says to the other: "I am sorry. Forgive me." That costs. Reconciliation. A marriage raised from the dead. A new life out of pain. A great mystery.

There is no explanation for any of these mysteries. No explanation that makes any sense. Why should a girl suddenly break down or a woman suddenly die or a marriage head for the rocks? There is no explanation that means anything. Knowing that a hidden disease had always been there, that a driver lost control of his car, or that there was not enough understanding in the marriage is not explanation enough. Knowledge is not enough. Knowledge may even make the situation worse. Knowledge sometimes puffs up.

Love builds up. When you love, you build. When you love, you accept. That is the first step from death to resurrection—to accept the breaking, accept the death, accept the pain, accept the adultery. To accept—that is a cross. Out of that acceptance comes the beginning of a new life.

Where is your life disjointed? Where is it not what it ought to be? Where is the responsibility you have that you wish you did not have? Where are your pains? Where is your cross?

When you accept that cross, it turns you outward toward other people—perhaps just toward one other person—and makes it possible for new life to come. You do not bring it on by an act of your will. It comes. A risen life always comes out of crucifixion, the acceptance of pain in love for another.

Of course it is a mystery. There are only one of two things you can do with a mystery. You can either accept it or reject it in very simple, concrete, human terms in your life just as it is. So you can begin to accept and to live the mystery of Christ's resurrection.

You know people who experience it. You have seen it. You have—in some way—already experienced it yourselves. If you have really engaged life and not given up, you have experienced resurrection.

So don't give up. Accept your cross—whatever it may be—and turn to another so that a resurrected life may begin to appear.

Then you can say, "I am risen. I am risen, indeed. Breaking and pain and dying have been turned to strength and wholeness, richness and graciousness of spirit. I am no longer eager to get my own way and be boss. I am reconciled to those I love no matter how dreadful the separation. The breaking and pain and dying have brought me into a new life, a resurrected life."

Then to say, "Christ is risen. He is risen, indeed" is to mean, God has raised me. This is what God is about.

This is God in Christ—raised from the dead.

That is God in me—raised from the dead.

God is risen; he is risen, indeed!

And lest you think that the resurrection of Christ is only a personal resurrection, let this also be said: When a people, a nation, can identify its cross, its involvement in pain—in causing pain and suffering pain—it, too, can be raised to a new national life. The way is exactly the same way: to accept that cross, to acknowledge its responsibility for that pain. To extend its concern for people other than its own and to let God raise it to heights of glory it has never known before—that is the way. If this nation would do that, then the whole world might cry, "He is risen; the Lord is risen, indeed."

13

The truth's superb surprise

"The letter killeth, but the spirit bringeth life."

II Corinthians 3:6

Literalism kills.
    The spirit brings life.
Literalism is idolatry.
    The spirit frees you from idols.
Literalism is the end.
    The spirit marks a new beginning.
Literalism lives in the past.
    The spirit lives in the present, pointing
        toward the future.
Literalism binds you to the dead past.
    The spirit frees you to live anew
        and to move into the future.

So when you search for the meaning of Easter, don't read the resurrection stories literally. That is a dead end. Literalism kills the story. Read them in the spirit—spiritually. Those stories are symbols revealing truth more true than literal facts. The Easter story is, to borrow a phrase from Emily Dickinson,

> . . . too bright for our infirm Delight
> the truth's superb surprise.

The "superb surprise" of the resurrection is not to be understood literally, but spiritually. To understand it only by trying to get at the historical facts kills the truth. But enter into the story with your spirit. Let your spirit carry you, introduce you, open the way for you to come to the mystery of "the truth's superb surprise." Let your spirit —that deep part of your nature where you know what's what, where your conscious and your unconscious mind overlap—let the spirit that dwells there be your guide.

If you read the resurrection story with your spirit, what you learn will be the truth that God wants you to understand now so that you may begin now to live a resurrected life, moving into the future with sure hope.

There is, in the depths of our being, a place where we touch *being* itself—where being itself grasps us. That borderline where our spirit rises from its psychic depths and moves toward our conscious mind, is, in fact, where we live our most real life. That deep inner spirit that rises from the depths of our being is hidden from other people, but it is more real than the external lives that they observe. Indeed, in the spirit, we can say that we are dead to all that external life already. Literal death, therefore, is nothing new. It is only a shadow, a passing fact which does not affect our real life. Our real life is already resurrected.

So, to live in the spirit is to begin to live a liberated life now. It is to begin to enter into the truth of Easter's "superb surprise." To move from dead facts of the past into the mystery of the present reality of your life is to begin to be resurrected. Let your spirit, therefore, be your guide into that truth which is God's truth told in the Easter story. Your spirit will appropriate whatever truth God's Spirit has prepared for you to live now.

So listen to St. Paul's description of the resurrection. Paul wrote in the spirit about the truth of the resurrection. If you listen to him in the spirit you will hear what God wants you to hear. Don't try to understand him literally; literalism kills. Listen to him with your spirit. This is what I hear when I listen to Paul in the spirit:

Some person will ask, "How are dead people raised up? What kind of bodies do they have?" Those are very foolish questions. The resurrected body is not like the physical body at all.

The physical body perishes; it dies just like a kernel of wheat dies. But out of the physical body there develops a spirit. That life of the spirit is the person. That spiritual body is the person in just the same way a person's spirit is the person. When you believe you know somebody, what you know is his spirit—you don't know his body. The spirit a person has is more important than his body.

You are surrounded with people and you say, "That person is a good person, and that person is a bad person; those people are lovely people, and those people are really pretty mean people." You are talking about those persons as they reveal their spirit. Their spirit is more real than their body. When we say, "Oh, I like him," or "Oh, I detest him," we are talking about his spirit; we are not talking about his physical body. His body may be beautiful and his spirit evil; or his body may be deformed and his spirit magnificent.

Where does glory come from? Who lifts you? You are lifted by the spirit of people. The physical body always returns to dust. Nobody can avoid that. But the spirit is not subject to physical death. The spirit transcends time and space. You have felt, haven't you, the impact of a person's spirit even though he lives a thousand miles away? You have known, haven't you, the impact of a person's spirit even though that person died fifty years ago? It is the spirit that endures, not the physical body.

Now I am going to tell you a mystery. I will let you in on a secret. When to the best of your ability you trust the spirit of love and try to obey it and express it in your life, you are living Christ's spirit. No, that is not quite it. Christ's spirit is living your spirit. You are clothed with Christ's spirit.

When that happens, then you do not have to worry anymore about how you are doing. You do not have to worry anymore about whether or not you are going to be able to fulfill all the cravings of your life. You do not have to worry anymore about what is going to happen to you. You do not have to spend any more energy making yourself secure against every contingency of life, against every awful thing that can happen to you—like death. You do not have to worry about that ever again. All that has been done away with by Christ.

You are free of that need to erect your defenses against the forces that come upon you. Those forces do not have any power anymore. You are free, in the spirit, to be absolutely yourself, because this is what the spirit, and the spiritual body, is all about. Therefore, while you are in the body, physically, go about your business. Live in that spirit as well as you can. Live day by day. Trust that spirit. Rejoice in that spirit. Exalt in that spirit. You already have that spiritual body that has clothed you. Do not worry about your physical body. And remember that everything you do in the spirit counts.

So then if you should ask again, "what about all those associations with people I have had in the spirit when I was in a physical body?" I will say: In the spirit, all things are yours—everything—all things, all people, all loves, every person whose spirit has been intertwined with your spirit. All of that is yours.

It does not make any difference how feeble those human loves have been; they are just the first loves of an infinitely greater love which shall possess you.

All things, all people, all loves—John and Mary, Peter and Jane—all things—the world, life, death, the present, the future—all are yours.

> And you are Christ's;
> and Christ is God's.

Do you hear the spirit saying something like this? Some "superb surprise"?

Literalism kills. The spirit brings life. Do not put your trust in the dead past. Put your trust in the living spirit—in your spirit. That is where you live.

Let your spirit, rising out of the depths of your being, lead you into the truth of Easter's "superb surprise." Trust your spirit to lead you into whatever truth God has prepared you to receive and to live in.

To live in that spirit is to live your life hid with Christ in God. You are dead to all the old. You are living a new life, a new resurrected life in the spirit—the truth's superb surprise.

14

The fabric of death and life

Life
Death
Eternal Life
Broken
Remade
Forever

Life and love are together. When they are broken and die they are re-created in new forms.

A forty-year-old man is describing the death of his wife. He says: "At three o'clock in the morning she just stopped breathing. When the nurse came, I left the room and walked down the hall. There was a broom. I picked it up and walked to the window. I put it to my shoulder and sighted along it as though it were a gun. I pointed it over the river toward New Jersey.

"Now," I thought, "are you going to pull the trigger and

be mad the rest of your life? No, that wasn't my wife. I am going to affirm her the rest of my life. She *is*. I put the broom down.

"She has continued to *be*—maybe even more powerfully than before she died." That is a reaction to the death of someone else.

Have you ever faced your own death? It dawned on a man that there would be a day when he would not be, and that after not many more days, it would be as though he had never been.

"The moment I was able to imagine the absolute obliteration of myself," he said, "I suddenly became nothing.

"Then when I looked around, not being anything, I became everything. Not having to make anything of myself, all things were at that moment given me. I became at one with the universe."

The acceptance of one's own death sometimes sets a person free to be wholly himself.

Have you thought about the death of God, or, more accurately, the death of your idea of God?

Every picture you had of him has faded, and then vanished:

—God as a man with a white beard;
—God as an angry father, or a kindly father;
—God who was in Jesus, but who perhaps never lived;
—God of power, who somehow never seemed to do anything;
—God of love, who permitted the loveless to torment the innocent;
—God of grace, who let men hate and destroy.

He suffered the little children to come unto him because there was no place they could lay their heads in safety. Nor is there yet.

Your gods die. Your pictures fail. God disappears. He is dead.

A man describes what happened when his god died. "When God died—when every picture of him was crumpled up and thrown away, and there was no God, and I didn't have to believe in my God—that was when I trusted him for the first time. He is beyond all knowing. When there was nothing, he came in everything.

"He came in the little children. He came in innocence. He came in every gift. In every human love, he came. He came in people's weakness. He came in the powerless. He came when hate had run its course and the tormenting spirit could prevail no longer.

"When I knew I no longer had to believe any picture of God—no picture of his power or his majesty or his sovereignty or his compassion or his loveliness or his grace—then I was able for the first time to believe in him.

"Thank God that God died. For now I know the God who is raised from the dead."

What shall we say to anyone who has experienced the death of someone they love, or the anticipation of their own death, or the death of their God? I would say at least three things:

1. You can't hold on. You can't hold on to those you love as though they were yours. You cannot possess another person, anybody's love, your own life, or your own God. They aren't yours.

2. Where there is love there is always hurt. At the heart of love there is always sacrifice. Built into the fabric of life and love is death and brokenness and sacrifice.

3. When death and sacrifice and brokenness are willingly accepted, a new life and a new love is given. The outer forms are different but the inner essence of living and loving is more powerful than ever.

The forms arising out of death are always life-affirming, love-affirming. They always go deeper into the mystery that is at the heart of things.

So we affirm a mystery. The mixture of life and love and death and sacrifice are forever. There will be new forms in a new life but they will affirm the essential love of God, who has been raised from the dead, and of all those who have been broken in him whose love will never die.

15

Easter comfort, Easter challenge

When the Coburn family moved to New York we left behind in Cambridge a collie dog who had been a member of our family for twelve years. His name was Laddie, a grandson of the TV star, Lassie, with the same coloring and the same style. We felt that it would be cruel to a dog of that age who had the free run of a campus in Cambridge to be locked up in an apartment in New York City except for supervised strolls through the park.

So we left him with a family in the country near Boston, a lovely family with children who loved Laddie as they loved their own dog and cat. We knew that they would take care of Laddie with as much affection and care as we would. One bitterly cold night in February he ran away. The next morning his footprints were tracked in the snow down to the woods near the river. There they were lost. No further trace has been found. We will not see Laddie again in this life.

Do you think that when we die we will see him?

If you have ever had a dog who has been a member of your family and who has ministered to you, you know how a dog comforts people. Do you think that you will see him again?

I do not know, but I hope so. Anybody who loves dogs hopes so. It seems to me a perfectly proper Christian hope that where love has bound God's creatures together, death does not break that relationship.

There is an old French prayer which goes like this:

> O God, my Master, should I gain the grace
> To see thee face to face when life is ended
> Grant that a little dog, who once pretended
> That I was God, may see me face to face.

The character of heaven must be such that at least it will honor the love that we have known on earth. God created every living creature—"and saw that it was good." The goodness of heaven must be at least as good as the goodness of earth.

St. John, in the last book in the Bible, is trying to say what the resurrection of Christ from the dead means. He has a vision. "I saw," he says, "a new heaven and a new earth. . . . I saw a holy city, . . . coming down out of heaven from God, . . . I heard a great voice . . . saying, 'Behold, the dwelling of God is with men. He will dwell with them and they shall be his people and God himself shall be with them; he will wipe away every tear from their eyes, and death shall be no more, neither shall there be mourning nor crying nor pain any more, for the former things have passed away.' "

A new heaven and a new earth together. A city coming out of heaven from God. A voice saying, "Behold, the dwelling of God is with men!"

So, while we are still on earth, heaven is a present

reality. It is not just a future hope. When we think of those we loved who have died, we think of them as still alive.

Peter T. Forsyth put it this way: "There are those who say when they follow their love into the unseen, 'I know that land. Some of my people live there. Some have gone on secret service which does not admit of communication but I meet from time to time the commanding officer and when I mention them to him he tells me that all is well!' "

When we mention them to him he tells us that "all is well" in heaven and in earth with those who love. Death is no more, there is no more mourning, no more crying, no more pain. Those former things are passed away now that Christ is raised from the dead. So we rejoice in the union and the reunion of love and its power to bring together all those relationships of love between people—even between people and dogs—all the creatures God has made and found good.

We take heart from St. John's vision of a new heaven and a new earth both at the same time. He saw a new heaven and a new earth together. The new heaven of love relationships exists on a new earth. It is not simply a new existence in another world beyond. Rather it is bound to this world. It is not heavenly love in the by and by. It is earthly love made heavenly in the here and now.

The Easter message brings both personal comfort and a social challenge. It says that heaven and earth are bound together and that the personal loves we believe will be fulfilled in heaven are but a part of that love in social relationships meant to exist on earth. John describes a city coming out of heaven, a city where the needs of *all* people are supplied, where their care and shelter and food, and the upbringing of their young, are important to the completion of God's creation. In John's new Jerusalem our personal love is translated into social concern and caring. It is a community where we get as exercised over young people lost on heroin as we do over our dogs who are lost.

Someone has said, "The city can only renew its hope if there are some people in it who will absorb the hatred and the tensions and transmute them into love." Who are more clearly called to do this than those who know that the Lord is risen and that there is, therefore, a new heaven and a new earth? Easter brings us both the comfort of knowing that our loves shall be re-created in heaven and the challenge to our loves of helping re-create the earth.

That re-creative heavenly love, I suppose, has been described nowhere more clearly than in those words of Martin Luther King speaking to his opponents: "We shall match your capacity to inflict suffering by our capacity to endure suffering. We shall meet your physical force with soul force. Do to us what you will and we shall continue to love you . . . One day we shall win freedom, but not only for ourselves: We shall so appeal to your heart and conscience that we shall win you in the process and our victory will be a double victory." [2]

May Easter comfort us when we think of Christ's victory in those whom we love. May it challenge us when we think of what his victory would mean for the life of our cities. Christ's victory must be a double victory—a new heaven and a new earth together.

16

Your share in the Ascension of Christ

And what the dead had no speech for, when living,
They can tell you, being dead. The communication
of the dead is tongued with fire
beyond the language of the living." [3]

T. S. ELIOT, "LITTLE GIDDING"

The communication of the dead is tongued with fire beyond the language of the living. When we let the voices of the dead speak to us with those tongues of fire, we are helped to view life from a sharper, clearer perspective. They give us a voice from another world which encompasses our own, and strengthens us to live more deeply in our own.

Think of someone in your life who has loved you and been genuinely concerned about you, preferably someone who has lived his life and has died and you have never

133

forgotten. Take a parent, or a grandparent, someone who has loved you who belongs to an older generation and who is no longer here in the flesh but is still part of you in the spirit. Have you ever reflected upon how you, in response to his spirit, begin to take upon yourself something of the same spirit?

Perhaps you can remember your father, for example, when you were small. He picked you up when you were hurt. You were comforted, and knew that you were safe in his arms, that whatever had happened was not going to hurt you any more. You were depending on the arms of someone who was stronger than you. You were safe.

As you grew older you came to learn that your father expected something from you. He expected a certain kind of behavior, a certain sense of values, a certain integrity. You gradually learned that what he expected of you he also expected of himself; that he never asked of you more than he asked of himself. He never asked you to do something contrary to what he believed and lived.

If he loved you he undoubtedly judged you. When you violated a trust that had been given you, when you betrayed the integrity that had come to be expected of you, when you no longer acted in a decent way, or when you acted without concern for anybody, he judged you for this kind of behavior. He also judged himself by the same standards. You and he were under the same judgment. You discovered that what he expected of you was a standard that apparently came from beyond himself. He was under a constraint to be loyal to something higher, just as he expected you to be loyal to the standards that he set for you. In this relationship you were becoming a person, becoming someone distinctively yourself, in response to his distinct person, in a relationship of authority, dependence, forgiveness, and reassurance.

As you grew up, you probably responded to him by both accepting his spirit and rejecting it. Sometimes you affirmed everything that your father stood for, sometimes you denied it; sometimes you were happy with it, sometimes unhappy. But in any case, whether accepting or rejecting or in whatever proportion of both, you were becoming yourself. He helped you become yourself as he revealed himself.

When you became an adult you began to look at him more objectively as an equal. You began to wonder more about him in himself. What made him the person he was? Who had shared his life significantly? What were the dreams he had for himself? Where were his failures? Where were his loyalties? What did he count on? What were his loves? Where had he betrayed love? It is fascinating to reflect upon the inner life of someone who has loved you.

He may have shown you, in fact, more of himself by the way he dealt with his defeats than the way he dealt with his victories. You may have discovered deeper and deeper insights into him in the way he met disappointment or frustration or failure than in the way he met success. If he was a great person, he probably met both with the same spirit—open, affirmative, not taking great pride in himself, modest, thankful for others, happy to honor others, grateful for living.

Even in his sickness, when sickness came, he revealed himself. Perhaps especially in his sickness, and in the way he met his death, he revealed himself. He may have met that final event with the same spirit with which he met everything else in life. Indeed some people say, "I never really understood who my father was, or understood how he loved me, until after he had died. It was then, maybe years later, that I began to get insights into what he was about and what the spirit that was in him had meant to me. I know now that spirit and him in a way I never did before."

So, think about that person or those persons who, by

their life, death, and the spirit by which they lived and
died, revealed themselves to you and thereby helped
make you in some measure who you are today.

Can you identify that spirit, the spirit that has, in love,
brought you under judgment, lifted you, and forgiven
you? Can you remember whose spirit made you strong
because of the expectations that were held out before you
as to who you might become? Whose spirit inspired in
you some measure of love and sacrifice, of compassion
and integrity and concern for other human beings?

That spirit is eternal and never fails. Everything else
fails—dishonesty, lying, corruption, unfaithfulness, self-
service—those all fail. Love never fails. That is what a
person's life is about. You live it and already you are
living eternal life.

This kind of statement is validated in part by our own
experiences. On a deeper level, it is validated by the
person of Jesus Christ and his experience.

An eternal quality is revealed in Christ's life; in his
decisions, in how he met failure as success, defeat as well
as victory. He revealed himself through his spirit, and
that spirit continued and continues.

Those who knew him in the flesh discovered that his
spirit of obedience to love was perfectly consistent
throughout his life and in the way he met death—and it
was validated by the resurrection. His ascension com-
pletes the story of his life, death, and resurrection. The
ascension symbolizes his eternal victory and the eternal
life of those who share his spirit. Ascended into heaven,
eternally united with love in the universe, he reigns as
Lord of the universe, never to be destroyed by any power
set against him.

The story of Jesus' ascension is an open-ended one. We
share in it as we live in his spirit and his spirit lives in us.

We are his presence in the world now. We continue to
do his work transforming the world as we live out of his

spirit of love and justice. Ascended into glory, he lives with us in our relations with one another, in our work and worship, and in our inner lives as we permit him to remake us in his image. His continuing life is our hope of glory. As we live in and with his spirit now we already share the power of his resurrection and ascension.

17
Rejoice in the Lamb

Rejoice in God, O ye Tongues; give the glory to the Lord, and the Lamb
Nations, and languages, and every Creature, in which is the breath of Life.
Let man and beast appear before him, and magnify his name together.

For I will consider my Cat Jeoffry
For he is the servant of the Living God, duly and daily serving him.
For at the first glance of the glory of God in the East he worships in his way.
For this is done by wreathing his body seven times round with elegant quickness.
For he knows that God is his Saviour.
For God has blessed him in the variety of his movements.
For there is nothing sweeter than his peace when at rest.

For I am possessed of a cat, surpassing in beauty,
from whom I take occasion to bless
Almighty God.

—CHRISTOPHER SMART

To "Rejoice in the Lamb" we need no special gifts. We need only ordinary human experiences. To live through ordinary human experiences and try to affirm ourselves and the people around us is to affirm God and to praise him. That is to "Rejoice in the Lamb."

Ask yourself: What are those ordinary experiences in my life that have prompted me to rejoice? When have I said, "When I went through that experience, I really rejoiced"?

A student might answer, "I really rejoiced when I finished school or passed that examination or did that paper." A young person might say, "I really rejoiced when, for the first time in my life, I fell in love, when I rejoiced in the existence of another human being." An adult might say, "I rejoiced when I finally delivered what I know I am able to deliver in life, when I accomplished something." An artist might say he rejoiced in his creation; a musician in her song, a poet in those polished words which finally fell into place and sounded as they were meant to sound. A parent might say, "I rejoiced in my children. I rejoiced in what they accomplished. I rejoiced in their joys. I rejoiced in them even when I did not rejoice in everything that they did or said. I rejoiced in them."

You can answer the question on the basis of your own experience. What are those experiences that cause you to look at life and to say, "I rejoice in it. I am fulfilled in it. There was a surging of life that went through me and I knew that I was. In that fact of being I was creating and rejoicing." That is to "Rejoice in the Lamb."

But it is more than that. It is also to look at those experiences that do not cause you to rejoice, those experiences that have made you say, "I will never again rejoice in anything." Have you ever had your heart lifted by the beauty of a sunset and the world of nature, and then had it dragged down as you see the destruction wrought by an earthquake? Have you ever laughed and played with someone over the years, someone you have loved, and then looked upon that person when he was dead? Have you ever left the happy sounds of young people and adults ice skating on a clear winter evening and gone from there to a hospital ward for the violently disturbed? Have you ever known anyone who has committed suicide? Have you ever thought of it yourself?

Have you ever felt absolutely at one with somebody or in a circle of friends, and then had a series of rejecting experiences which made you feel that you were not together with anyone but utterly alone?

After you have had a deep sense of the presence of God, have you ever felt that it was all just in your mind, that God was dead, if indeed he had ever lived?

These questions are important because if we are to rejoice—really rejoice—somehow we have to rejoice in *all* of life, the entire creation to which we belong, and not simply in certain selected pleasant experiences which make us happy. We are meant to celebrate existence, life, everything that has been created, our whole life.

To do that, we need help. We obviously cannot do it by ourselves. How can I celebrate the death of someone I love? How can I praise ugliness which destroys beauty? There is too much in life set against rejoicing. It is asking life to do something it cannot possibly do—to provide the resources for rejoicing. The facts of life are too much for life to bear. We need help.

One of the helps is music—not all music by a long shot —but good music that rises out of the depths of human experiences, the tragic as well as the joyful. Indeed the greatest music, the most powerful music, the music that moves people most is the music that has risen out of suffering, pain, tragedy, and all the terrible experiences of life. That kind of music lifts the soul, drives out anxieties and fears, and sets life in a framework of nobility. Music —real music—is of help because it identifies, accepts, transforms by its spirit all the experiences of life. So there is a grandeur in the life that we share when we are transported by music.

The words at the beginning of this chapter are from *A Festival Cantata*, composed by Benjamin Britten after a poem by Christopher Smart. Smart was a man who experienced the worst of life. Beginning in his early thirties, after a youth of great promise, he experienced failure after failure, poverty, lack of recognition, probably alcoholism, and certainly emotional and mental break-down. Still, in his moments of sanity he can write "Rejoice in the Lamb." How extraordinary that is!

The Lamb symbolizes innocent suffering—that spirit which takes all the best and all the worst in life and sacrifices itself because it loves another. In ancient ritual that goes back to the dawn of history, the lamb is offered as a sacrifice to join the mystery of God and the mystery of man together. When God and men are together, rather than separated or opposed, then all life—the worst as well as the best—can be affirmed.

The Lamb is Christ, who was sacrificed from before the foundation of the world, eternally, so that men might know God is with them, loving them forever. At the heart of creation, embedded in the fabric of life, is this divine love. This powerful innocent love prevails. The Lamb—innocent love sacrificing itself—prevails. Rejoice in the Lamb! God is praised by the worst as by the best. The sacrifice at the heart of life is love.

Now the final question: Is it true? Or is it sentiment?

Can you count on it? Or is it an ideal that soon blows away? You have to answer the question from your life as you reflect upon all your experiences. When you have needed help most, where has it come from? Has it not come, generally speaking, from those who have themselves suffered? It has not come from the protected ones, but from the involved ones. It has not come from people who are superficially happy, but from those who have been broken. Isn't it generally true that when you are down and out, the people who come into your life with power are the ones who know what you are going through because they have been through those same things? They have come out on the other side stronger than when they went in and they say, "This can happen to you too. If you want strength, go to it. It's there." That strength is the Lamb.

During the last three years of his life the former Presiding Bishop of the Episcopal Church, Arthur Lichtenberger, was a professor at the Episcopal Theological School where I was then serving. He had resigned as Presiding Bishop because he was suffering from Parkinson's disease. During those three years he became increasingly disabled, shuffled rather than walked, mumbled rather than talked, pointed rather than wrote. The more disabled he became physically, the more powerful his spirit became in that community. Curious! The strength seemed just to emanate from him.

One winter morning I was in my study feeling depressed. (February in Cambridge can be pretty depressing.) I was going through one of those moods that we all go through, just feeling sorry for myself. I happened to look out the window, and there up the road, shuffling along on those icy paths, came Bishop and Mrs. Lichtenberger, arm in arm. Just as I looked at them there came a surge of strength, almost as if I were experiencing a rebirth. All I could do was to rejoice in them. That is to rejoice in the Lamb. That is his work. That is where the strength for living is.

Curious, isn't it, how strength comes. Even more than knowledge, pain is power. "In love's service," says Thornton Wilder, "only the wounded can serve." Where you see the wounded, you see the Lamb. Where you are wounded is where you can serve and rejoice in him.

This is not to rejoice in suffering; it is to rejoice in him who transforms suffering into power, and therefore to rejoice in all of life. That is the song that the Lamb sang before creation. That is the song expressed in the cross. That is the song that we sing in our own lives.

We can hear it in those words with which Christopher Smart closes his text:

> For the trumpet of God is a blessed
> intelligence and so are all the instruments in Heaven.
> For God the father Almighty plays upon the
> harp of stupendous magnitude and melody.
> For at that time malignity ceases and
> the devils themselves are at peace.
> For this time is perceptible to man by
> a remarkable stillness and serenity of soul.
> Hallelujah from the heart of God and from
> the hand of the artist inimitable
> And from the echo of the heavenly harp in
> sweetness magnifical and mighty.

Therefore, Rejoice in the Lamb!

18

Christ our Passover

*C*hrist our Passover is sacrificed for us:
   therefore let us keep the feast.
What we could not do, he has done,
   therefore let us eat, drink, sing for joy.

Not with old leaven, neither with
   the leaven of malice and wickedness.
No sir, not with our old ways,
   not with self-will, self-pity, self,
   self, self; neither with meanness,
   conniving, cunning, and the calculating eye,

But with the unleavened bread of
   sincerity and truth.
Yes, sir. From now on our word our bond;
   we say what we mean—straight out;
   we call them as we see them;
   Yea, yea or nay, nay.

Christ being raised from the death dieth no more;

144

death hath no more dominion over him.
He did it once. Once and for all.
All done. Not again. Never again.
No more in the hands of evil men.
No more under the dominion of anyone
    but his Father.
All that separates him from his Father
    dead and gone,
    withered away,
    burned, tossed
    in the ashcan,
    rubble,
    finished,
    kaput.

For in that he died, he died unto sin once:
    but in that he liveth, he liveth unto God.
Made sin. He who knew no sin, made sin for us.
Made man. Made man for us.
    To be made man, made sin
    naturally,
How else be man except be sin?
Broken body, broken sin, flesh dead, dead to sin
    once, once and for all. That's all. Dead and
    done.
Living now, living in love, in God, to God, for God.
    God himself. Just being himself.
    No more dying.
    Only living
    Being
    Loving
    living and loving
    being God. God being.
    Eternally. Forever and
    ever and ever and ever.
    Being. God. Living. Loving.

Likewise reckon ye also yourselves to be dead
    indeed unto sin, but alive unto God
    through Jesus Christ our Lord.
So, therefore, . . . because of this of course
        therefore. . . .
    It follows that as a consequence, there-
        fore. . . .
Likewise. . . . The same way. Just because he did
    do you, too, are dead to self; no more "I,"
    "I," "I," "me," "me," "me," no more
    self-love . . . self-will . . . self-pity . . .
        self-service
    all dead, buried, gone forever into the grave.
Alive now, up, resurrected, up and at 'em
    new hope,
    new love,
    new zip, bang, purpose, zest
    and joy
Carried now—no more carrying
    possessed now—no more possessions
    to put our faith in, be burdened by,
    encumbered by,
    weighed down by
    houses and trunks of stuff,
    treasures you can't take with you
    or junk without end.
    No more, dead, buried.
Now, alive, free
    to be yourself.
    Just yourself.
    Free
    to be in God,
    in life, in love
    forever and ever and ever,
    through Jesus Christ our Lord.

Christ is risen from the dead, and become
the first-fruits of them that slept.
For since by man came death, by man
also came the resurrection of the dead.
So all creation sings to praise you,
    creator of sun and moon
    stars, galaxies, atoms, and cells
    all things of earth, green things, growing things,
    grass, water and fire,
    pebbles and wind,
    rain and weather,
    lilies of the field,
    flowers that burst from
    the womb of the universe.
All live in
    dying, praising living,
    dying again, praising and living again,
    world without end, resurrected,
    bursting, being because they are,
    just because they are
    they praise you.

For as in Adam all die, even so in Christ
shall all be made alive.
Despair is dead,
    all deceits, ill will and any
    purpose served in bombs dropping,
    falling, exploding—all dead and gone.
Death is dead.
    God has destroyed death;
    all set against him, is gone
    tears flowing, hands touching,
    tongues touching,
    separations,
    goings and comings
    in pain and joy.

All this is dead, gone, finished
　　forever—finally.
For now we live in him,
　　stand fast against that which stands in our way,
　　no more cowardice, fear, anxiety, thrashing
　　　around—
　　just steadfast.
We are alive in him.
　　one in him—we are because we are—
　　we praise him.
So,
When Christ our Passover
　　is sacrificed for us.
　　let us keep the feast
　　eating, drinking, singing with joy.

Glory be to the Father, and to the Son,
　　and to the Holy Ghost;
As it was in the beginning,
　　is now,
　　and ever shall be,
　　world without end!

Amen.

Notes and Acknowledgments

PREFACE

1. Søren Kierkegaard, *The Sickness Unto Death* (New York: Anchor Books, 1954); combined with *Fear and Trembling*, translated by Walter Lowrie.

PART I: IN LIFE

1. Reprinted by permission of Charles Scribner's Sons from *The Wind in the Willows* by Kenneth Grahame. Copyright 1908 by Charles Scribner's Sons; also Methuem & Co., London, England.

2. William Blake, "Gnomic Verses, XVII" in *The Poetical Works of William Blake* (New York: Oxford University Press, 1958).

3. Kahlil Gibran, *The Prophet*. Reprinted with permission of the publisher, Alfred A. Knopf, Inc. Copyright © 1923 by Kahlil Gibran: renewal copyright © 1951 by Administrators C.T.A. of Kahlil Gibran Estate and Mary G. Gibran, pp. 83–86.

4. Robert Coles, *Migrants, Sharecroppers, and Mountaineers*, Vol. II of *Children of Crisis* (Boston: Atlantic-Little, Brown, 1972), pp. 579–586.

149

5. From "St. Patrick's Breastplate" translated by Cecil Frances Alexander, The Hymnal 1940, no. 269.

6. Dag Hammarskjöld, *Markings* (New York: Alfred A. Knopf, Inc., 1973), p. 165.

7. William Blake, "Several Questions Answered (Eternity)" in *The Poetical Works of William Blake* (New York: Oxford University Press, 1958), p. 196.

8. Robert Penn Warren, "I Am Dreaming Of A White Christmas: The Natural History of a Vision" from *Or Else— Poems/Poems 1968–1974*. Reprinted with permission of the publisher, Random House, Inc. Copyright © 1974 by Robert Penn Warren, p. 22; also William Morris Agency, N.Y.

PART II: IN DEATH

1. Kurt Vonnegut, Jr., *Slaughterhouse-Five* (New York: Delacorte Press, 1969), p. 182.

PART III: IN RESURRECTION

1. Lyrics from the following songs from GODSPELL: "We Beseech Thee," "Save The People," "Day By Day," and "O Bless The Lord, My Soul"—Copyright © 1971 Music of the Times Publishing Corp. (Valando Music Division) and New Cadenza Music Corporation. All rights administered by Music of the Times Publishing Corporation. Used by permission. All rights reserved. Permission also granted by EMI Music Publishing Ltd. The passage beginning "There once was a rich man . . ." from the book of GODSPELL used by permission of the authors, John-Michael Tebelak and Stephen Schwartz.

2. Martin Luther King, *Strength to Love, Collected Sermons* (New York: Harper & Row, 1963), pp. 48–49.

3. From "Little Gidding" in *Four Quartets* by T.S. Eliot, copyright 1943 by Esme Valerie Eliot. Reprinted by permission of Harcourt Brace Jovanovich, Inc.; also Faber & Faber Ltd., London, England.